新丝路"中文+职业技能"系列教材编写委员会
（中文+景点导游）

总策划：郁云峰　谢永华
策　划：于天琪　孙雁飞

总主编：谢永华　杜曾慧
语言类主编：杜曾慧
专业类主编：何正英
语言类副主编：朱金兰　严　峻　王　茜　史其慧

顾　问：朱志平　林秀琴　宋继华

项目组长：陈维昌
项目副组长：付彦白
项目成员：武传霞　赫　栗　张　彪

▶ 新丝路"中文+职业技能"系列教材
New Silk Road "Chinese + Vocational Skills" Series

中文+景点导游
Chinese + Sightseeing Guide

新丝路"中文+职业技能"系列教材编写委员会 编

© 2024 北京语言大学出版社，社图号 24185

图书在版编目（CIP）数据

中文＋景点导游 / 新丝路"中文＋职业技能"系列教材编写委员会编． -- 北京：北京语言大学出版社，2024.12． -- ISBN 978-7-5619-6664-8

Ⅰ．H195.4；F590.63

中国国家版本馆 CIP 数据核字第 2024GM3510 号

中文＋景点导游
ZHONGWEN + JINGDIAN DAOYOU

排版制作：	北京创艺涵文化发展有限公司
责任印制：	周 燚
出版发行：	北京语言大学出版社
社　　址：	北京市海淀区学院路 15 号，100083
网　　址：	www.blcup.com
电子信箱：	service@blcup.com
电　　话：	编 辑 部　8610-82303647/3592/3724
	国内发行　8610-82303650/3591/3648
	海外发行　8610-82303365/3080/3668
	北语书店　8610-82303653
	网购咨询　8610-82303908
印　　刷：	北京富资园科技发展有限公司
版　　次：	2024 年 12 月第 1 版　　**印　次：** 2024 年 12 月第 1 次印刷
开　　本：	889 毫米 × 1194 毫米　1/16　　**印　张：** 11.75
字　　数：	239 千字
定　　价：	98.00 元

PRINTED IN CHINA

凡有印装质量问题，本社负责调换。售后 QQ 号 1367565611，电话 010-82303590

编写说明

新丝路"中文+职业技能"系列教材是把中文作为第二语言，结合专业和职业的专门用途、职业用途的中文教材，不是专业理论教材，不是一般意义的通用综合中文教材。本系列教材定位为职场生存中文教材、立体式技能型语言教材。教材研发的目标是既要满足学习者一般中文环境下的基本交际需求，又要满足学习者职业学习需求和职场工作需求。它和普通的国际中文教材的区别不在语法，而在词汇的专门化程度，在中文的用途、使用场合、应用范围。目前，专门用途、职业用途的中文教材在语言分类和研究成果上几近空白，本系列教材的成功研发开创了中文学习的新视野、新领域、新方向，将"中文+职业技能+X等级证书"真正融合，使学习者在学习中文的同时，也可通过实践掌握职业技能，从而获得X等级证书。

适用对象

1. HSK4级左右的学生，来华学习中文和职业技能的长期生或短期进修生。
2. 海内外导游专业的中文学习者。
3. 海外有意从事导游专业工作的中文学习者。

教材结构

本教材采取专项语言技能与职业技能训练相结合的中文教学及教材编写模式，配有专业视频教学资源，还附有"视频脚本""参考答案"等配套资源。

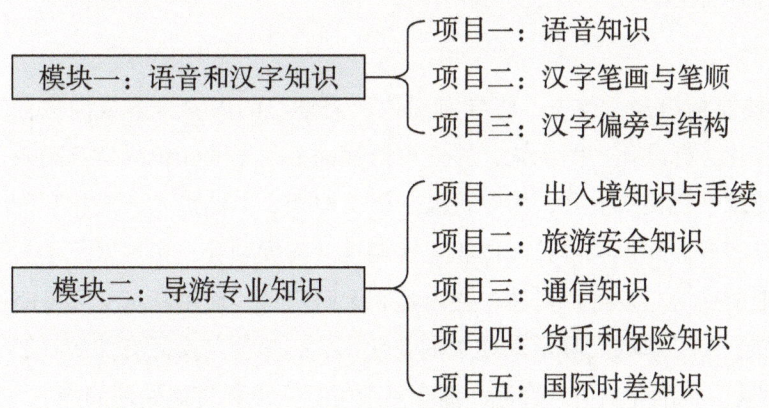

模块三：我未来的工作
- 项目一：景区接待服务
- 项目二：景区解说服务
- 项目三：景区商业服务
- 项目四：其他辅助服务
- 项目五：景点导游词

模块四：工作坊实训
- 项目一：景区接待实训
- 项目二：景区解说实训
- 项目三：景区购物服务实训
- 项目四：其他辅助服务实训
- 项目五：景点导游词讲解实训

编写理念

将"中文＋职业技能"融入在工作场景对话中，把工作分解成一个个任务，用图片认知方法解决词汇的认知问题，用视频展示的方法解决学习者掌握中文词汇与专业技能的不匹配问题，注重技能的实操性，注重"在做中学"。模块二中的每个项目都设置"学以致用"板块，目的不仅仅是解决任务中的词汇认知问题，更是将学习的目标放在"能听""能用""能模仿说出"上。我们力争通过大量图片和配套视频，将教材打造成立体式技能型语言教材，方便学习者更好地自主学习。

教材目标

将中文与导游的职业技能相结合。首先，将导游岗位所需学习的内容分解成岗位任务。然后，将岗位任务程序化、标准化、图示化，并使得语言词汇与专业知识科学、高效复现，语言水平与专业技能水平螺旋式上升，情景阶段、语义框架、本体输入方式相互配合。最后，使汉语学习、导游专业知识学习及岗位职业技能提升高度融合，实现以下学习目标：能听懂工作场合一般的交谈与发言，抓住主要内容和关键信息，使用基本交际策略与他人交流，开展工作；能初步了解与交际活动相关的文化因素，掌握与交际有关的一般文化背景知识；能进行流程化、标准化的信息交流；拥有复杂信息交流和特情处理的能力。

编写原则

1. 语言知识技能与专业知识技能并进，满足当前热门的、急需急用的岗位需求。

2. 渐进分化，综合贯通，拆解难点，分而治之。

3. 语言知识与专业知识科学、高效复现，语言技能与专业技能螺旋式上升，职场情境、语义框架、本体输入方式相互配合。

4. 使用大量的图片和视频，实现专业知识和技能呈现形式可视化。

5. 强化专业岗位实操性技能。本系列教材配有专业技术教学的视频，突出展示专业岗位的实操性技能，语言学习难度与技能掌握难度的不匹配可通过实操性强的视频和实训环节来补充。

使用建议

1. 本教材共有四个模块，分别为语音和汉字知识、导游专业知识、我未来的工作和工作坊实训，可以依据学习者的汉语及专业水平确定相应的课时，选择模块学习。

2. 注释和说明着力于简明、扼要，教材注重实操性，注重听说，涉及到的语法知识，教师可视情况予以细化和补充。

3. "工作坊实训"可以在课文和语言点学完之后作为课堂练习使用，建议模拟完成。教师要带领学生一步步按照专业要求完成，专业实操需要教师的引领操作，实现技能学习的目标。

4. 项目小结是对整个项目关键词汇和核心内容的总结，通过这个部分的听说练习，可以更好地了解本项目的核心工作任务。

5. 教师上课时要充分利用教材所设计的练习，多听多练，听说结合，学做合一。

6. 教师带领学习者熟练诵读课文，要求学习者把每课的关键词汇、句子和导游常用语背诵下来。

特别感谢

感谢教育部中外语言交流合作中心将新丝路"中文＋职业技能"系列教材列为重点研发项目，为我们教材编写增添了动力和责任感。教材编写委员会负责整套教材的规划、设计与编写协调，并先后召开上百次讨论会，对每册教材的课文编写、体例安排、注释说明、练习设计、图片选择、视频制作等进行全方位的评估、讨论和审定。感谢编写委员会成员和所有编者高度的敬业精神、精益求精的编写态度，以及所投入的热情和精力、付出的心血与智慧。感谢关注本系列教材并贡献宝贵意见的国际中文教育教学界专家和全国各地的同人。

Compilation Instructions

The New Silk Road "Chinese +Vocational Skills" is a series of Chinese textbooks that uses Chinese as a second language for specialized and vocational purposes. It is not a professional or theoretical textbook, nor is it a general comprehensive Chinese textbook. Instead, it is a series of Chinese textbooks for workplace survival and development of comprehensive skills. It aims not only to meet learners' basic communication needs in a general Chinese environment, but also their needs for vocational learning and work. It differs from ordinary international Chinese textbooks not in grammar, but in the specialization of vocabulary, and the purpose, occasions, and scope of Chinese language use. At present, there is almost no language classification and research findings of Chinese textbooks for specialized and vocational purposes. The successful launch of this series opens up new horizons, new fields, and new directions for Chinese learning and truly integrates Chinese, vocational skills, and X-level certificates. It makes a student to master vocational skills and obtain an X-level certificate while studying Chinese.

Target users

1. Students passing HSK level 4 or above, and long-term or short-term students studying Chinese and vocational skills in China.

2. Chinese language students majoring in tour guiding in China and the rest of the world.

3. Overseas Chinese language students who are interested in working as tour guides.

The structure of Chinese + Textbook for Tour Guiding

This series of textbooks integrates the training of specialized language skills and vocational skills when teaching Chinese language and writing the textbooks. It has professional video teaching resources, "video scripts", "reference answers", and other supporting resources.

Module 1: Knowledge on Phonetics and Chinese Characters
Item 1: Phonetic Knowledge
Item 2: Strokes and Stroke Orders of Chinese Characters
Item 3: Radicals and Structures of Chinese Characters

Module 2 Tour Guide Expertise

Item 1: Knowledge and Procedures for Exit and Entry

Item 2: Knowledge on Travel Safety

Item 3: Knowledge on Communication

Item 4: Knowledge on Currency and Insurance

Item 5: Knowledge on International Time Difference

Module 3 My Future Job

Item 1: Reception Service at Scenic Spots

Item 2: Commentary Service at Scenic Spots

Item 3: Commercial Service at Scenic Spots

Item 4: Other Supporting Service

Item 5: Tour Commentaries for Scenic Spots

Module 4 Practical Training at Workshops

Item 1: Simulation of Reception at Scenic Spots

Item 2: Simulation of Commentaries at Scenic Spots

Item 3: Simulation of Shopping Service at Scenic Spots

Item 4: Simulation of Other Supporting Service

Item 5: Simulation of Delivering Tour Commentaries

Writing ideas

It integrates Chinese and vocational skills into the dialogues at workplaces and breaks down a job into tasks. It uses pictures to recognize and learn vocabulary and uses videos to solve the mismatch between students' mastery of Chinese vocabulary and professional skills, emphasizing the practicability of skills and "learning by doing". Each item in Module 2 has a "Practicing What You Have Learnt" section, which not only aims to recognize and learn the vocabulary in this item, but also aims to be able to listen to it, to use it, to imitate it, and to speak it out. We strive to develop comprehensive skill-based language textbooks through a large number of pictures and supporting videos and provide convenience for self-taught learners.

Objectives of the textbooks

It combines Chinese with tour guides' professional skills. First, it breaks down what a tour guide needs to learn into tasks. Then, it programs, standardizes, and illustrates the tasks, making the vocabulary and vocational knowledge scientifically and efficiently recur, one's language proficiency and professional skills spiral up, and the situational stage, semantic framework, and ontology input methods cooperate with each other. Finally, to highly integrate one's learning of Chinese, learning of tour guide expertise and enhancement of vocational skills, one needs to realize the following objectives: to be able to understand the general conversations and speeches in workplaces, learning the major content and key information; to be able to use the basic communication strategies to communicate with others and do the work; to be able to gain a preliminary understanding of cultural factors related to communication activities and learn the general cultural background information related to communication; to be able to make procedural and standardized communication; and to be able to communicate complicated information and deal with special situations.

Writing principles

Language knowledge skills and professional skills go hand in hand to meet the demands of present-day popular and urgently needed jobs;

1. It makes progressive differentiation and comprehensive integration, breaking down the difficult points and teaching them one by one;

2. Language knowledge and professional knowledge recur scientifically and efficiently, language skills and professional skills spiral upward, and the situational stage, semantic framework, and ontology input methods cooperate with each other;

3. It visualizes the professional knowledge and skills through a lot of pictures and videos;

4. It strengthens the practical skills in professional positions. This series of textbooks has the corresponding video on professional skills, which highlights the practical skills of professions. The mismatch between the difficulty in learning a language and difficulty in mastering skills can be supplemented by the video and training.

Suggestions for use

1. Each textbook has four modules, i.e., Knowledge on Phonetics and Chinese Characters, Tour Guide Expertise, My Future Job, and Practical Training at Workshops. Students can decide the corresponding class hours and choose the modules they are going to study based on their Chinese and professional proficiency.

2. The notes and explanations are simple and concise. The textbooks put emphasis on practicality and stress on listening and speaking. Teachers can elaborate and supplement the grammar involved depending on the circumstances.

3. The "Practical Training at Workshops" section can be used as classwork after studying the texts and language points. It is suggested to be completed through simulation. Teachers need to help students complete it step by step following the vocational requirements and provide guidance in the professional operation to help students learn skills.

4. The "Item Summary" section summarizes the key vocabulary and core content of the unit. After taking listening and speaking exercises in this section, one can better understand the core tasks of the unit.

5. In class, teachers should make full use of the exercises in the textbook, listening and practicing as much as possible with the integration of listening and speaking, and learning and practice.

6. The teacher helps students read aloud the text proficiently, asking them to memorize the key vocabulary, sentences, and common expressions used by tour guides in each lesson.

Acknowledgements

We are grateful to the Center for Language Education and Cooperation of the Ministry of Education for listing the New Silk Road "Chinese + Vocational Skills" series as a key research and development project, which enhances our motivation and sense of responsibility to textbook compilation. The Textbook Compilation Committee is responsible for the planning, design, compilation, and coordination of the whole series of textbooks, and has held hundreds of meetings to conduct comprehensive evaluation, discussion, and approval of textbook compilation, style arrangement, notes and explanations, exercise design, picture selection, and video production of each textbook. We'd like to express our gratitude to members of the Compilation Committee and all compilers for their professional dedication, unwavering pursuit of perfection in the compilation, as well as their enthusiasm, effort, hard work and wisdom. Our thanks also go to the experts in international Chinese language education and colleagues from all over the country who have kept a close eye on this series and contributed their valuable opinions.

语法术语及缩略形式参照表
Abbreviations of Grammar Terms

Grammar Terms in Chinese	Grammar Terms in Pinyin	Grammar Terms in English	Abbreviations
名词	míngcí	noun	n.
专有名词	zhuānyǒu míngcí	proper noun	pn.
代词	dàicí	pronoun	pron.
数词	shùcí	numeral	num.
量词	liàngcí	measure word	m.
数量词	shùliàngcí	quantifier	q.
动词	dòngcí	verb	v.
助动词	zhùdòngcí	auxiliary	aux.
形容词	xíngróngcí	adjective	adj.
副词	fùcí	adverb	adv.
介词	jiècí	preposition	prep.
连词	liáncí	conjunction	conj.
助词	zhùcí	particle	part.
拟声词	nǐshēngcí	onomatopoeia	onom.
叹词	tàncí	interjection	int.
前缀	qiánzhuì	prefix	pref.
后缀	hòuzhuì	suffix	suf.
成语	chéngyǔ	idiom	idm.
短语	duǎnyǔ	phrase	phr.
主语	zhǔyǔ	subject	S
谓语	wèiyǔ	predicate	P
宾语	bīnyǔ	object	O
定语	dìngyǔ	attributive	Attrib
状语	zhuàngyǔ	adverbial	Adverb
补语	bǔyǔ	complement	C

CONTENTS 目录

模块一　语音和汉字知识　Knowledge on Phonetics and Chinese Characters　1

项目一　语音知识　Phonetic Knowledge　1
项目二　汉字笔画与笔顺　Strokes and Stroke Orders of Chinese Characters　11
项目三　汉字偏旁与结构　Radicals and Structures of Chinese Characters　17

模块二　导游专业知识　Tour Guide Expertise　31

项目一　出入境知识与手续　Knowledge and Procedures for Exit and Entry　31
　　一、热身 Warm-up　32
　　二、课文 Texts　34
　　三、视听说 Viewing, Listening, and Speaking　37
　　四、学以致用 Practicing What You Have Learnt　38
　　五、小知识 Tips　39
　　项目小结 Item Summary　40

项目二　旅游安全知识　Knowledge on Travel Safety　42
　　一、热身 Warm-up　42
　　二、课文 Texts　44
　　三、视听说 Viewing, Listening, and Speaking　47
　　四、学以致用 Practicing What You Have Learnt　49
　　五、小知识 Tips　51
　　项目小结 Item Summary　52

项目三　通信知识　Knowledge on Communication　53
　　一、热身 Warm-up　53
　　二、课文 Texts　55
　　三、视听说 Viewing, Listening, and Speaking　58
　　四、学以致用 Practicing What You Have Learnt　59

I

	五、小知识 Tips	60
	项目小结 Item Summary	61
项目四	货币和保险知识 Knowledge on Currency and Insurance	63
	一、热身 Warm-up	63
	二、课文 Texts	65
	三、视听说 Viewing, Listening, and Speaking	68
	四、学以致用 Practicing What You Have Learnt	69
	五、小知识 Tips	70
	项目小结 Item Summary	71
项目五	国际时差知识 Knowledge on International Time Difference	73
	一、热身 Warm-up	73
	二、课文 Texts	74
	三、视听说 Viewing, Listening, and Speaking	78
	四、学以致用 Practicing What You Have Learnt	79
	五、小知识 Tips	80
	项目小结 Item Summary	81

模块三　我未来的工作　My Future Job　83

项目一	景区接待服务 Reception Service at Scenic Spots	83
	流程与规范 Procedures and Specifications	84
	工作模块一 Working Module 1	86
	工作模块二 Working Module 2	88
	工作模块三 Working Module 3	91
项目二	景区解说服务 Commentary Service at Scenic Spots	96
	流程与规范 Procedures and Specifications	96
	工作模块一 Working Module 1	99
	工作模块二 Working Module 2	101
	工作模块三 Working Module 3	104
项目三	景区商业服务 Commercial Service at Scenic Spots	107
	流程与规范 Procedures and Specifications	107
	工作模块一 Working Module 1	109
	工作模块二 Working Module 2	111
	工作模块三 Working Module 3	115
项目四	其他辅助服务 Other Supporting Service	117
	流程与规范 Procedures and Specifications	118
	工作模块一 Working Module 1	120

工作模块二 Working Module 2		122
工作模块三 Working Module 3		125

项目五　景点导游词　Tour Commentaries' for Scenic Spots … 128

流程与规范 Procedures and Specifications		129
工作模块一 Working Module 1		130
工作模块二 Working Module 2		133
工作模块三 Working Module 3		136
工作模块四 Working Module 4		140

模块四　工作坊实训　Practical Training at Workshops … 143

项目一　景区接待实训　Simulation of Reception at Scenic Spots		143
项目二　景区解说实训　Simulation of Commentaries at Scenic Spots		144
项目三　景区购物服务实训　Simulation of Shopping Service at Scenic Spots		145
项目四　其他辅助服务实训　Simulation of Other Supporting Service		146
项目五　景点导游词讲解实训　Simulation of Delivering Tour Commentaries		147

附录　Appendixes … 148

导游常用语 100 句　100 Common Expressions Used by Tour Guides		148
词语总表　Vocabulary		155
视频脚本　Video Scripts		160
参考答案　Reference Answers		162

1

Yǔyīn hé hànzì zhīshi
语音和汉字知识
Knowledge on Phonetics and Chinese Characters

项目一　Item 1

语音知识　Phonetic Knowledge

一

1. 声母和韵母（1）　Initials and finals (1)

（1）声母表　Table of initials

声母 Initials	国际音标 International Phonetic Alphabet	声母 Initials	国际音标 International Phonetic Alphabet	声母 Initials	国际音标 International Phonetic Alphabet
b	[p]	g	[k]	zh	[tʂ]
p	[pʰ]	k	[kʰ]	ch	[tʂʰ]
m	[m]	h	[x]	sh	[ʂ]
f	[f]	j	[tɕ]	r	[ʐ]
d	[t]	q	[tɕʰ]	z	[ts]
t	[tʰ]	x	[ɕ]	c	[tsʰ]
n	[n]			s	[s]
l	[l]				

（2）韵母表　Table of finals

韵母 Finals	开口呼韵母 Open-mouth Finals	齐齿呼韵母 Even-teeth Finals	合口呼韵母 Closed-mouth Finals	撮口呼韵母 Round-mouth Finals
单韵母 Single Finals	-i[ɿ]、-i[ʅ]	i[i]	u[u]	ü[y]
	a[A]	ia[iA]	ua[uA]	
	o[o]		uo[uo]	
	e[ɤ]			
	er[ər]	ie[iɛ]		üe[yɛ]

1

（续表）

韵母 Finals	开口呼韵母 Open-mouth Finals	齐齿呼韵母 Even-teeth Finals	合口呼韵母 Closed-mouth Finals	撮口呼韵母 Round-mouth Finals
复韵母 Compound Finals	ai[ai]		uai[uai]	
	ei[ei]		uei[uei]	
	ao[ɑu]	iao[iɑu]		
	ou[ou]	iou[iou]		
鼻韵母 Finals with a Nasal Consonant or Consonants	an[an]	ian[iɛn]	uan[uan]	üan[yan]
	en[ən]	in[in]	uen[uən]	ün[yn]
	ang[ɑŋ]	iang[iɑŋ]	uang[uɑŋ]	
	eng[əŋ]	ing[iŋ]	ueng[uəŋ]	
			ong[uŋ]	iong[yŋ]

2. 声调图　Figure of tones

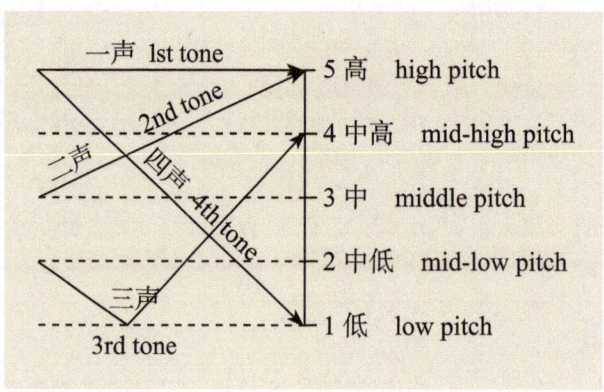

3. 读一读　Let's read　🎧 01-01

① guójì 国际　　② yǐngxiǎng 影响　　③ xiūxi 休息

④ shǐyòng 使用　　⑤ jiàgé 价格　　⑥ xìnyòngkǎ 信用卡

⑦ xiànjīn 现金　　⑧ bǎoxiǎn 保险　　⑨ lǐpéi 理赔

二

1. 音节　Syllables

汉语的音节一般由声母、韵母和声调组成，音节开头的辅音是声母，声母后面的部分是韵母，韵母上面的部分是声调。例如，在音节"nǐ"中，"n"是声母，"i"是韵母，"ˇ"是声调。音节也可以没有声母，只有韵母和声调，例如"é"。

语音和汉字知识
Knowledge on Phonetics and Chinese Characters

A Chinese syllable is usually composed of an initial, a final and a tone. The consonant that starts a syllable is called the initial, the part after the initial is the final, and the part above the final is the tone. For example, in the syllable "nǐ", "n" is the initial, "i" is the final, and "ˇ" is the tone. Syllables can also have no initials, only finals and tones, such as "é".

声母 Initials	韵母 Finals	声调 Tone	音节 Syllable
n	i	ˇ	nǐ
b	a	-	bā
d	ian	ˋ	diàn
h	ao	ˇ	hǎo
	e	ˊ	é

2. 声母和韵母（2） Initials and finals (2)

(1) 声母 Initials：b p m f d t n l g k h

声母 Initials	国际音标 International Phonetic Alphabet	声母 Initials	国际音标 International Phonetic Alphabet	声母 Initials	国际音标 International Phonetic Alphabet
b	[p]	d	[t]	g	[k]
p	[pʰ]	t	[tʰ]	k	[kʰ]
m	[m]	n	[n]	h	[x]
f	[f]	l	[l]		

(2) 开口呼韵母 Open-mouth finals

开口呼韵母 Open-mouth Finals	国际音标 International Phonetic Alphabet	开口呼韵母 Open-mouth Finals	国际音标 International Phonetic Alphabet	开口呼韵母 Open-mouth Finals	国际音标 International Phonetic Alphabet
-i	[ɿ]	ai	[ai]	an	[an]
-i	[ʅ]	ei	[ei]	en	[ən]
a	[ᴀ]	ao	[ɑu]	ang	[ɑŋ]
o	[o]	ou	[ou]	eng	[əŋ]
e	[ɤ]				
er	[ɚ]				

3. 声调 Tones

汉语是有声调的语言，声调不同，意义就可能不一样。

汉语普通话有四个基本声调。标识声调的符号有四个："-"表示第一声，"ˊ"表示第二声，"ˇ"表示第三声，"ˋ"表示第四声。调号标在主要元音的上边，例如：mā、má、mǎ、mà。

Chinese is a tonal language. Different tones may result in different meanings.

There are four basic tones in Mandarin Chinese. They are marked as "ˉ" (the 1st tone), "ˊ" (the 2nd tone), "ˇ" (the 3rd tone), and "ˋ" (the 4th tone) respectively. Tones are marked above the main vowel. For example, "mā", "má", "mǎ", "mà".

4. 读一读 Let's read 01-02

① bǎozhèngjīn 保证金　　② xìnyòng édù 信用 额度　　③ bǎoxiǎn 保险

④ fùkuǎn 付款　　⑤ qīxiàn 期限　　⑥ bǎoguǎn 保管

⑦ yōngdǔ 拥堵　　⑧ duìhuàn 兑换　　⑨ hùzhàohào 护照号

三

1. 声母和韵母（3） Initials and finals (3)

（1）声母 Initials：zh ch sh r z c s

声母 Initials	国际音标 International Phonetic Alphabet	声母 Initials	国际音标 International Phonetic Alphabet
zh	[tʂ]	z	[ts]
ch	[tʂʰ]	c	[tsʰ]
sh	[ʂ]	s	[s]
r	[ʐ]		

（2）合口呼韵母 Closed-mouth finals

合口呼韵母 Closed-mouth Finals	国际音标 International Phonetic Alphabet	合口呼韵母 Closed-mouth Finals	国际音标 International Phonetic Alphabet	合口呼韵母 Closed-mouth Finals	国际音标 International Phonetic Alphabet
u	[u]	uai	[uai]	uang	[uɑŋ]
ua	[uA]	uei	[uei]	ueng	[uəŋ]
uo	[uo]	uan	[uan]	ong	[uŋ]
		uen	[uən]		

2. 轻声 Neutral tone

汉语里有些音节不带声调，念得又短又轻，拼写时不标号，这种念得又短又轻的声调叫轻声。例如：爸爸（bàba，dad）、妈妈（māma，mom）。

语音和汉字知识
Knowledge on Phonetics and Chinese Characters

Some syllables in Chinese don't have tones and are pronounced short and lightly, which are known as neutral tone. For example, "爸爸" (bàba, dad), "妈妈" (māma, mom).

3. 读一读 Let's read 🎧 01-03

① xiūxi 休息　　② xíngli 行李　　③ zhīshi 知识

④ zěnme 怎么　　⑤ xièxie 谢谢　　⑥ wèi shénme 为什么

四

1. 声母和韵母（4） Initials and finals (4)

（1）声母 Initials：j q x

声母 Initial	国际音标 International Phonetic Alphabet	声母 Initial	国际音标 International Phonetic Alphabet	声母 Initial	国际音标 International Phonetic Alphabet
j	[tɕ]	q	[tɕʰ]	x	[ɕ]

（2）齐齿呼、撮口呼韵母 Even-teeth finals and round-mouth finals

齐齿呼韵母 Even-teeth finals

齐齿呼韵母 Even-teeth Final	国际音标 International Phonetic Alphabet	齐齿呼韵母 Even-teeth Finals	国际音标 International Phonetic Alphabet	齐齿呼韵母 Even-teeth Finals	国际音标 International Phonetic Alphabet
i	[i]	ia	[iA]	ian	[iɛn]
		ie	[iɛ]	in	[in]
		iao	[iɑu]	iang	[iɑŋ]
		iou	[iou]	ing	[iŋ]

撮口呼韵母 Round-mouth finals

撮口呼韵母 Round-mouth Final	国际音标 International Phonetic Alphabet	撮口呼韵母 Round-mouth Final	国际音标 International Phonetic Alphabet	撮口呼韵母 Round-mouth Finals	国际音标 International Phonetic Alphabet
ü	[y]	üe	[yɛ]	üan	[yan]
				ün	[yn]
				iong	[yŋ]

2. 听读辨音 Listen, read and discriminate the pronunciation. 🎧 01-04

j—zh　　　　　q—ch　　　　　x—sh
ju—zhu　　　qu—chu　　　xu—shu

ji—zhi	qi—chi	xi—shi
jie—zhe	qian—chan	xian—shan
jia—zha	qiao—chao	xie—she
jin—zhen	qin—chen	xing—sheng
jiu—zhou	qing—cheng	xiang—shang

3. 听读辨调　**Listen, read and discriminate the tones**　🎧 01-05

yuè—yuē	jiā—jià	qī—qǐ	xué—xuè
yǔ—yú	jiǔ—jiù	qián—qiǎn	xī—xǐ
yīng—yǐng	jīn—jǐn	qù—qǔ	xiè—xiě
yòu—yǒu	jìng—jīng	qǐng—qīng	xíng—xìng
yān—yán	jiāng—jiàng	qiū—qiú	xiǎo—xiào

4. 读一读　**Let's read**　🎧 01-06

① jiàgé 价格　　② qítā 其他　　③ xìnyòngkǎ 信用卡

④ jiānkòng 监控　　⑤ jīngcǎi 精彩　　⑥ xiànjīn 现金

⑦ yājīn 押金　　⑧ yìyuàn 意愿　　⑨ jùjué 拒绝

五

1. 拼音规则（1）　Spelling rules (1)

i、u、ü 单独构成音节时，分别写作 yi、wu、yu。

When "i", "u" or "ü" forms a syllable by itself, the syllable is respectively written as yi, wu, and yu.

2. 三声变调　Third-tone sandhi

两个三声音节连读时，前一个三声声调读二声。例如：

When a third-tone syllable is followed by another third-tone syllable, the third tone in the first syllable is pronounced as the second tone. For example:

nǐ hǎo 读作 ní hǎo　　　　　　　　Fǎyǔ 读作 Fáyǔ

3. "不"的变调　Tone sandhi of "不"

"不"本调是第四声。"不"在第一声、第二声、第三声前面时，声调不变；在第四声前面时，读第二声。例如：

The original tone of "不" is the fourth tone. The tone doesn't change when "不" is followed by a first-tone, second-tone or third-tone syllable, but it becomes the second tone when "不" is followed by a fourth-tone. For example:

不 bù + { 吃 chī / 来 lái / 好 hǎo / 是 shì } = { 不+吃 bù chī / 不+来 bù lái / 不+好 bù hǎo / 不+是 bú shì }

4. 读下面的词语，并在"bu"上边标上声调
   Read the following words put the tone marks above "bu" 🎧 01-07

   不喝 bu hē   不吃 bu chī   不多 bu duō
   不学 bu xué   不想 bu xiǎng   不小 bu xiǎo
   不买 bu mǎi   不看 bu kàn   不去 bu qù
   不对 bu duì   不累 bu lèi   不要 bu yào
   不漂亮 bu piàoliang 不客气 bu kèqi   不上网 bu shàngwǎng
   不新鲜 bu xīnxiān 不知道 bu zhīdào   不开门 bu kāimén

5. 读一读 **Let's read** 🎧 01-08

   ① dǎoyóu 导游   ② yǎnchū 演出   ③ liúliàng 流量
   ④ zhùyì 注意   ⑤ bàojǐng 报警   ⑥ xiāofèi 消费
   ⑦ bú zhùyì 不注意   ⑧ bú bàojǐng 不报警   ⑨ bù xiāofèi 不消费

六

1. 拼写规则（2） **Spelling rules (2)**

（1）以 i 开头的韵母自成音节时，除了 in、ing 前加 y 外，其他均是把 i 写作 y。

When finals starting with i form syllables on their own, i is written as y, except in in and ing, where y is added at the beginning.

ia→ya   ie→ye
iao→yao   iou→you
ian→yan   iang→yang
iong→yong
in→yin   ing→ying

（2）以 u 开头的韵母自成音节时，u 写作 w。

When finals starting with u form syllables on their own, u is written as w.

ua→wa   uo→wo

uai→wai   uei→wei
uan→wan   uen→wen
uang→wang ueng→weng

（3）以 ü 开头的韵母自成音节时，ü 前面加上 y，去掉 ü 上的两点。

When finals starting with ü form syllables on their own, y is used before ü, and the two dots above ü are removed.

üe→yue   üan→yuan   ün→yun

2. 读一读 Let's read 🎧 01-09

① wúzhèng tānfàn 无证 摊贩
② Jīnbiān Wánggōng 金边 王宫
③ wēixiǎn 危险
④ wàimiàn 外面
⑤ wèishēngjiān 卫生间
⑥ wàihuì 外汇
⑦ sān yuè 三月
⑧ yùnchē 晕车
⑨ yuánlín 园林

七

1. 拼写规则（3） Spelling rules(3)

ü 或者以 ü 开头的韵母跟 j、q、x 相拼的时候，省略 ü 上边的两点，写成 ju、qu、xu、jue、que、xue、juan、quan、xuan、jun、qun、xun。跟 n、l 相拼的时候，ü 上边的两点不能省略，写成 nü、lü、lüe、nüe。

When ü or a final beginning with ü is combined with j, q or x, the two dots above ü are removed and ü is written as u as in ju, qu, xu, jue, que, xue, juan, quan, xuan, jun, qun, xun. When combined with n or l, the two dots above ü cannot be removed. For example, nü, lü, lüe, and nüe.

2. "一"的变调 Tone sandhi of "一"

数词"一"本调是第一声。"一"后边的音节是第一声、第二声、第三声时，"一"读作"yì"；"一"后边的音节是第四声时，"一"读作"yí"。例如：

The original tone of the numeral 一 is the first tone. 一 is pronounced as yì when it is followed by a first-tone, second-tone or third-tone syllable. It is read as yí when it is followed by a fourth-tone syllable. For example:

一斤 yì jīn   一台 yì tái   一种 yì zhǒng   一个 yí gè

3. 读一读 Let's read 🎧 01-10

① jūzhùzhèng 居住证
② shíqū 时区
③ xūyào 需要

语音和汉字知识
Knowledge on Phonetics and Chinese Characters

④ xúnwèn 询问　　⑤ quēshǎo 缺少　　⑥ xuānchuán 宣传

⑦ yí cè 一册　　⑧ yì wǎn 一晚　　⑨ yì chē 一车

八

1. 拼写规则（4） Spelling rules (4)

iou、uei、uen 前面有声母时，写成 iu、ui、un。例如：
iou, uei or uen is written as iu, ui or un after an initial. For example:

n + iou → n + iu → niu

g + uei → g + ui → gui

l + uen → l + un → lun

2. 儿化　Erhua

卷舌元音 er 与其他韵母结合，使韵母带上卷舌色彩，这种现象称为"儿化"，卷舌的韵母称为"儿化韵"。"儿化"具有区别词义、区分词性和表示细小、轻松或亲切、喜爱的感情色彩的作用。儿化时，"儿"与前面的韵母读成一个音节。拼写时在前面韵母末尾加上"r"，汉字写法是在原来的汉字后边加"儿"。例如：

The combination of a retroflex vowel er with a final is called "*erhua*", and the final is called "*erhua* final". "*Erhua*" is used to discriminate word meanings and parts of speech, and express being very small, relaxed, or affectionate. The "*er*" at the end is pronounced together with the syllable before it. In spelling, an "r" is added to the end of the syllable before it, and "儿" is added to the end of the original Chinese character. For example:

nǎ + er → nǎr（哪儿）

zhè + er → zhèr（这儿）

3. 读一读 Let's read　🎧 01-11

① guīzé 规则　　② qìwēn 气温　　③ lúnchuán 轮船

④ niǔdài 纽带　　⑤ lùndiǎn 论点　　⑥ qīngguǐ 轻轨

⑦ míngpáir 名牌儿　　⑧ yìdiǎnr 一点儿　　⑨ liáotiānr 聊天儿

九

1. 拼写规则（5）：隔音符号的用法　Spelling rules (5): the usage of the syllable-dividing mark

a、o、e 开头的音节连接在其他音节后边的时候，如果音节的界限发生混淆，要使用隔音符号"'"隔开。例如：

When a syllable beginning with a, o, or e comes after another syllable and there is ambiguity in the boundaries of syllables, the syllable-dividing mark " ' " is used. For example,

xī + ān → xiān（先）　　Xī'ān（西安）

pí + ǎo → piǎo（漂）　　pí'ǎo（皮袄）

2. 读一读　Let's read　 01-12

① fāng'àn 方案　　② fān'àn 翻案　　③ kù'ài 酷爱

④ yú'é 余额　　⑤ dàng'àn 档案　　⑥ yòu'éryuán 幼儿园

十

1. 声调的标写　Marking of tones

声调标写在一个音节的主要元音上，按照 a、o、e、i、u、ü 的先后顺序标调。韵母 iu、ui 的声调标在后一个元音上，声调标在 i 上面时，i 上的小点要省去。例如：

The tone mark is written above the main vowel of a syllable. The tone is marked according to the following order: a, o, e, i, u, ü. For the vowels iu and ui, the tone mark is written above the latter vowel. When the tone mark is placed on i, the dot on the top of i is omitted. For example:

dà 大　　mén 门　　duō 多　　lèi 累　　xué 学　　shuǐ 水　　niú 牛　　xīn 心

2. 读一读　Let's read　 01-13

① dìzhǐ 地址　　② lǐpéi 理赔　　③ ānquán 安全

④ shěnchá 审查　　⑤ qīxiàn 期限　　⑥ shēnglǐ 生理

⑦ bǎoxiǎn 保险　　⑧ shǒudū 首都　　⑨ ānpái 安排

项目二　Item 2
汉字笔画与笔顺　Strokes and Stroke Orders of Chinese Characters

一

1. 汉字的笔画（1）　Strokes of Chinese characters (1)

笔画 Strokes	名称 Names	例字 Examples
一	横 héng	二
丨	竖 shù	十
丿	撇 piě	人
丶	捺 nà	八

2. 汉字的笔顺（1）　Stroke orders of Chinese characters (1)

规则 Rules	例字 Examples	笔顺 Stroke orders
先横后竖 Horizontal strokes before vertical strokes	十	一 十
先撇后捺 Left-falling strokes before right-falling strokes	人 八	丿 人 丿 八

3. 认读下列词语，并试着读写构成词语的汉字　Recognize the following words, and try to read and write the Chinese characters forming these words

二

1. 汉字的笔画（2）　Strokes of Chinese characters (2)

笔画 Strokes	名称 Names	例字 Examples
丶	点 diǎn	六
𠃍	横折 héngzhé	口、日、五
𡿨	竖折 shùzhé	山
㇜	撇折 piězhé	么

2. 汉字的笔顺（2） Stroke orders of Chinese characters (2)

规则 Rules	例字 Examples	笔顺 Stroke orders
先上后下 Upper strokes before lower strokes	三	一 二 三
先左后右 Left-side strokes before right-side strokes	人	丿 人

3. 认读下列词语，并试着读写构成词语的汉字 Recognize the following words, and try to read and write the Chinese characters forming these words

liù yuè　shénme　rìyòng　shānjǐng
六月　什么　日用　山景

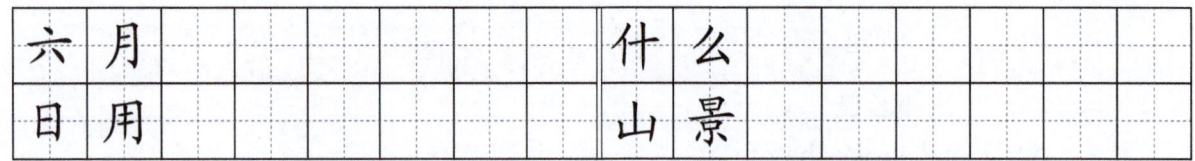

三

1. 汉字的笔画（3） Strokes of Chinese characters (3)

笔画 Strokes	名称 Names	例字 Examples
㇆	横钩 hénggōu	买
亅	竖钩 shùgōu	小
乚	弯钩 wāngōu	子
㇗	竖弯钩 shùwāngōu	七

2. 汉字的笔顺（3） Stroke orders of Chinese characters (3)

规则 Rules	例字 Examples	笔顺 Stroke orders
先中间后两边 Strokes in the middle before those on both sides	小	亅 小 小
先外边后里边 Outside strokes before inside strokes	问	丶 冂 门 问 问 问

语音和汉字知识 1
Knowledge on Phonetics and Chinese Characters

3. 认读下列词语，并试着读写构成词语的汉字 Recognize the following words, and try to read and write the Chinese characters forming these words

mǎimai　érzi　qī yuè　xiǎohuǒr
买卖　儿子　七月　小伙儿

买	卖					儿	子					
七	月					小	伙	儿				

四

1. 汉字的笔画（4） Strokes of Chinese characters (4)

笔画 Strokes	名称 Names	例字 Examples
⼂	提 tí	习
⼂	竖提 shùtí	衣
⼂	横折提 héngzhétí	语
⼂	撇点 piědiǎn	女

2. 汉字的笔顺（4） Stroke orders of Chinese characters (4)

规则 Rule	例字 Examples	笔顺 Stroke orders
先外后里再封口 Outside strokes before inside strokes, and then sealing strokes	国 日	丨 冂 冂 冃 围 国 国 国 丨 冂 月 日

3. 认读下列词语，并试着读写构成词语的汉字 Recognize the following words, and try to read and write the Chinese characters forming these words

xísú　yīfu　yǔyán　guójí
习俗　衣服　语言　国籍

习	俗					衣	服					
语	言					国	籍					

13

五

1. 汉字的笔画（5）Strokes of Chinese characters (5)

笔画 Strokes	名称 Names	例字 Examples
㇂	斜钩 xiégōu	我
㇃	卧钩 wògōu	心
㇆	横折钩 héngzhégōu	问
㇈	横折弯钩 héngzhéwāngōu	几

2. 汉字的结构（1）Structures of Chinese characters (1)

结构类型 Structure type	例字 Examples	结构图示 Illustration
独体结构 Independent structure	生 不	□

3. 认读下列词语，并试着读写构成词语的汉字 Recognize the following words, and try to read and write the Chinese characters forming these words

wǒmen　xīnyuàn　wènhǎo　jǐ gè
我们　心愿　问好　几个

我	们					心	愿				
问	好					几	个				

六

1. 汉字的笔画（6）Strokes of Chinese characters (6)

笔画 Strokes	名称 Names	例字 Examples
㇌	横撇弯钩 héngpiěwāngōu	部
㇋	横折折折钩 héngzhézhézhégōu	奶

2. 汉字的结构（2）Structures of Chinese characters (2)

结构类型 Structure type	例字 Example	结构图示 Illustration
品字形结构 品-shaped structure	品	⊟

语音和汉字知识 1
Knowledge on Phonetics and Chinese Characters

3. 认读下列词语，并试着读写构成词语的汉字 Recognize the following words, and try to read and write the Chinese characters forming these words

bùmén	niúnǎi	pǐncháng	pǐnwèi
部门	牛奶	品尝	品位

部	门					牛	奶				
品	尝					品	位				

七

1. 汉字的笔画（7） Strokes of Chinese characters (7)

笔画 Strokes	名称 Names	例字 Examples
ㄅ	竖折折钩 shùzhézhégōu	马
ㄟ	横折斜钩 héngzhéxiégōu	风

2. 汉字的结构（3） Structures of Chinese characters (3)

结构类型 Structure types	例字 Examples	结构图示 Illustrations
上下结构 Top-bottom structure	爸 节	日
上中下结构 Top-middle-bottom structure	意	目

3. 认读下列词语，并试着读写构成词语的汉字 Recognize the following words, and try to read and write the Chinese characters forming these words

mǎshàng	fēngjǐng	xuéxí	yìsi
马上	风景	学习	意思

马	上					风	景				
学	习					意	思				

15

八

1. 汉字的笔画（8） Strokes of Chinese characters (8)

笔画 Strokes	名称 Names	例字 Examples
ㄴ	竖弯 shùwān	四
ㄟ	横折弯 héngzhéwān	没

2. 汉字的结构（4） Structures of Chinese characters (4)

结构类型 Structure types	例字 Examples	结构图示 Illustrations
左右结构 Left-right structure	银 饭	⊟
左中右结构 Left-middle-right structure	班 微	⊞

3. 认读下列词语，并试着读写构成词语的汉字 Recognize the following words, and try to read and write the Chinese characters forming these words

sìjì　mòshōu　yínháng　fàndiàn
四季　没收　银行　饭店

四 季　　　　　　没 收
银 行　　　　　　饭 店

九

1. 汉字的笔画（9） Strokes of Chinese characters (9)

笔画 Strokes	名称 Names	例字 Examples
㇆	横折折撇 héngzhézhépiě	延、建
㇉	竖折撇 shùzhépiě	专

2. 汉字的结构（5） Structures of Chinese characters (5)

结构类型 Structure types	例字 Examples	结构图示 Illustrations
全包围结构 Fully-enclosed structure	国	□

语音和汉字知识
Knowledge on Phonetics and Chinese Characters

（续表）

结构类型 Structure types	例字 Examples	结构图示 Illustrations
半包围结构 Semi-enclosed structure	医 边 问 唐 凶	

3. 认读下列词语，并试着读写构成词语的汉字 Recognize the following words, and try to read and write the Chinese characters forming these words

yùnyíng　dàolù　zhuānmén　yīyuàn
运营　道路　专门　医院

运	营					道	路				
专	门					医	院				

项目三　Item 3
汉字偏旁与结构 Radicals and Structures of Chinese Characters

一

1. 汉字的偏旁（1） Radicals of Chinese characters (1)

偏旁 Radicals	例字 Examples	部件组合 Combinations	结构图示 Illustrations
口	吗 呢 哪 吃 啊 叫	口＋马 口＋尼 口＋那 口＋乞 口＋阿 口＋丩	
囗	国 图	囗＋玉 囗＋冬	

17

偏旁 Radicals	例字 Examples	部件组合 Combinations	结构图示 Illustrations
女	妈	女+马	⊟
	她	女+也	⊟
	姓	女+生	⊟
	娜	女+那	⊟
亻	你	亻+尔	⊟
	他	亻+也	⊟
	们	亻+门	⊟
	作	亻+乍	⊟
	什	亻+十	⊟
	做	亻+故	⊟
日	时	日+寸	⊟
	晚	日+免	⊟
	明	日+月	⊟
	早	日+十	吕
	星	日+生	吕

2. 认读下列词语，并试着读写构成词语的汉字 Recognize the following words, and try to read and write the Chinese characters forming these words

nǎlǐ　xìngmíng　shíchā　jiànkāng shēnmíngkǎ
哪里　姓名　时差　健康 申明卡

哪	里					国	籍				
姓	名					时	差				
健	康	申	明	卡							

语音和汉字知识
Knowledge on Phonetics and Chinese Characters

二

1. 汉字的偏旁（2） Radicals of Chinese characters (2)

偏旁 Radicals	例字 Examples	部件组合 Combinations	结构图示 Illustrations
氵	汽 法 汉 洗 澡 没	氵+气 氵+去 氵+又 氵+先 氵+桌 氵+殳	
讠	语 课 请 谢 词 谁 认 识	讠+吾 讠+果 讠+青 讠+射 讠+司 讠+隹 讠+人 讠+只	
艹	节 英 花 苹 蕉	艹+卩 艹+央 艹+化 艹+平 艹+焦	
辶	远 这 运 道	辶+元 辶+文 辶+云 辶+首	
辶	边 选 还	辶+力 辶+先 辶+不	

19

2. 认读下列词语，并试着读写构成词语的汉字 Recognize the following words, and try to read and write the Chinese characters forming these words

yóulǎn	shèshī	róngxìng	dǐdá	yùnyíngshāng
游览	设施	荣幸	抵达	运营商

浏	览						设	施				
荣	幸						抵	达				
运	营	商										

二

1. 汉字的偏旁（3） Radicals of Chinese characters (3)

偏旁 Radicals	例字 Examples	部件组合 Combinations	结构图示 Illustrations
扌	打	扌+丁	▯▯
	拾	扌+合	▯▯
	报	扌+艮	▯▯
	找	扌+戈	▯▯
	排	扌+非	▯▯
	搬	扌+般	▯▯
木	树	木+对	▯▯
	机	木+几	▯▯
	极	木+及	▯▯
	杯	木+不	▯▯
	校	木+交	▯▯
	样	木+羊	▯▯
纟	经	纟+至	▯▯
	红	纟+工	▯▯
	绿	纟+录	▯▯
	绒	纟+戎	▯▯

语音和汉字知识 1
Knowledge on Phonetics and Chinese Characters

（续表）

偏旁 Radicals	例字 Examples	部件组合 Combinations	结构图示 Illustrations
心	怎	乍+心	
	想	相+心	
	态	太+心	
	感	咸+心	
	您	你+心	
足	路	足+各	
	跟	足+艮	
	踢	足+易	
	跑	足+包	

2. 认读下列词语，并试着读写构成词语的汉字 Recognize the following words, and try to read and write the Chinese characters forming these words

yājīn　xiāngchà　jiǎonà　gǎnxiè
押金　相差　缴纳　感谢

| 押 | 金 | | | | | 相 | 差 | | | |
| 缴 | 纳 | | | | | 感 | 谢 | | | |

四

1. 汉字的偏旁（4） Radicals of Chinese characters (4)

偏旁 Radicals	例字 Examples	部件组合 Combinations	结构图示 Illustrations
阝（左）	阿	阝+可	
	院	阝+完	
	陪	阝+音	

21

（续表）

偏旁 Radicals	例字 Examples	部件组合 Combinations	结构图示 Illustrations
宀	宿 家 安 室 客 字 定	宀+佰 宀+豕 宀+女 宀+至 宀+各 宀+子 宀+疋	
又	对 难 欢 友	又+寸 又+隹 又+欠 ナ+又	
月	朋 服 脑 期	月+月 月+艮 月+𡿺 其+月	
钅	银 错 钱 钟	钅+艮 钅+昔 钅+戋 钅+中	
王	玩 现 球 班	王+元 王+见 王+求 王+丿+王	

语音和汉字知识 1
Knowledge on Phonetics and Chinese Characters

2. 认读下列词语，并试着读写构成词语的汉字 Recognize the following words, and try to read and write the Chinese characters forming these words

qīxiàn	zhùsù	yǒuhǎo	fúwù	xiànjīn	yínhángkǎ
期限	住宿	友好	服务	现金	银行卡

期	限					住	宿			
友	好					服	务			
现	金					银	行	卡		

五

1. 汉字的偏旁（5） Radicals of Chinese characters (5)

偏旁 Radicals	例字 Examples	部件组合 Combinations	结构图示 Illustrations
巾	帽	巾 + 冒	
	帮	邦 + 巾	
	带	卅 + 冖 + 巾	
广	店	广 + 占	
	床	广 + 木	
	麻	广 + 林	
	应	广 + 业	
小	少	小 + 丿	
丷	光	丷 + 兀	
	当	丷 + 彐	
	尝	丷 + 冖 + 云	
八	分	八 + 刀	
	公	八 + 厶	
	共	卄 + 八	
	兴	丷 + 八	
	典	曲 + 八	

23

（续表）

偏旁 Radicals	例字 Examples	部件组合 Combinations	结构图示 Illustrations
刂	到	至 + 刂	☐☐
	刻	亥 + 刂	☐☐
	别	另 + 刂	☐☐
	制	制 + 刂	☐☐

2. 认读下列词语，并试着读写构成词语的汉字 Recognize the following words, and try to read and write the Chinese characters forming these words

shāngdiàn　dàodá　quánlì　gōnggòng
商店　到达　全力　公共

| 商 | 店 | | | | | | 到 | 达 | | | | |
| 全 | 力 | | | | | | 公 | 共 | | | | |

六

1. 汉字的偏旁（6） Radicals of Chinese characters (6)

偏旁 Radicals	例字 Examples	部件组合 Combinations	结构图示 Illustrations
竹	笔	竹 + 毛	☐
	篮	竹 + 监	☐
	箱	竹 + 相	☐
	等	竹 + 寺	☐
	管	竹 + 官	☐
	简	竹 + 间	☐
	第	竹 + 弟	☐
灬	然	狀 + 灬	☐
	点	占 + 灬	☐
	热	执 + 灬	☐
	黑	黒 + 灬	☐
	照	昭 + 灬	☐

语音和汉字知识
Knowledge on Phonetics and Chinese Characters

（续表）

偏旁 Radicals	例字 Examples	部件组合 Combinations	结构图示 Illustrations
衤	衬	衤+寸	
	衫	衤+彡	
	裤	衤+库	
雨	需	雨+而	
	雪	雨+彐	
	零	雨+令	
土	城	土+成	
	地	土+也	
	场	土+旸	
	坏	土+不	
	去	土+厶	

2. 认读下列词语，并试着读写构成词语的汉字 Recognize the following words, and try to read and write the Chinese characters forming these words

qiānfā　bǎoguǎn　xūyào　tiánxiě　zūlìndiǎn
签发　　保管　　需要　　填写　　租赁点

签	发					保	管				
需	要					填	写				
租	赁	点									

七

1. 汉字的偏旁（7）Radicals of Chinese characters (7)

偏旁 Radicals	例字 Examples	部件组合 Combinations	结构图示 Illustrations
走	超	走+召	
	趣	走+取	
	起	走+己	
	趟	走+尚	

25

偏旁 Radicals	例字 Examples	部件组合 Combinations	结构图示 Illustrations
忄	忙	忄+亡	☐☐
	快	忄+央	☐☐
	慢	忄+曼	☐☐
	惯	忄+贯	☐☐
	情	忄+青	☐☐
攵	教	孝+攵	☐☐
	收	丩+攵	☐☐
	数	娄+攵	☐☐
	放	方+攵	☐☐
饣	馆	饣+官	☐☐
	饭	饣+反	☐☐
	饺	饣+交	☐☐
	饼	饣+并	☐☐
	饿	饣+我	☐☐
禾	和	禾+口	☐☐
	种	禾+中	☐☐
	租	禾+且	☐☐
	季	禾+子	☐☐

2. 认读下列词语，并试着读写构成词语的汉字 Recognize the following words, and try to read and write the Chinese characters forming these words

cānyǐn gǎnjǐn shùliàng jìjié
餐饮 赶紧 数量 季节

| 餐 | 饮 | | | | | | | 赶 | 紧 | | | | | | |
| 数 | 量 | | | | | | | 季 | 节 | | | | | | |

语音和汉字知识
Knowledge on Phonetics and Chinese Characters

八

1. 汉字的偏旁（8） Radicals of Chinese characters (8)

偏旁 Radicals	例字 Examples	部件组合 Combinations	结构图示 Illustrations
门	问	门 + 口	
	闻	门 + 耳	
	间	门 + 日	
	闹	门 + 市	
疒	病	疒 + 丙	
	瘦	疒 + 叟	
冂	网	冂 + 㐅	
	同	冂 + 㝸	
	冈	冂 + 乂	
车	辆	车 + 两	
	轻	车 + 巠	
	较	车 + 交	
	辅	车 + 甫	
贝	费	弗 + 贝	
	赛	寨 + 贝	
	贵	㬰 + 贝	

2. 认读下列词语，并试着读写构成词语的汉字 Recognize the following words, and try to read and write the Chinese characters forming these words

wǎngluò　xiāofèi　tānfàn　bǐjiào　wèishēngjiān
网络　消费　摊贩　比较　卫生间

网络　　　　　　消费
摊贩　　　　　　比较
卫生间

27

九

1. 汉字的偏旁（9） Radicals of Chinese characters (9)

偏旁 Radicals	例字 Examples	部件组合 Combinations	结构图示 Illustrations
耳	聊	耳 + 卯	⊟
	职	耳 + 只	⊟
	取	耳 + 又	⊟
	联	耳 + 关	⊟
欠	歌	哥 + 欠	⊟
	歉	兼 + 欠	⊟
	欢	又 + 欠	⊟
冫	冷	冫 + 令	⊟
	准	冫 + 隹	⊟
	次	冫 + 欠	⊟
彳	行	彳 + 丁	⊟
	得	彳 + 昙	⊟
	律	彳 + 聿	⊟
	很	彳 + 艮	⊟

2. 认读下列词语，并试着读写构成词语的汉字 Recognize the following words, and try to read and write the Chinese characters forming these words

huānyíng　zhǔnbèi　lǚxíng　liáotiānr
欢迎　　准备　　旅行　　聊天儿

| 欢 | 迎 | | | | | | 准 | 备 | | | | | |
| 旅 | 行 | | | | | | 聊 | 天 | 儿 | | | | |

语音和汉字知识 1
Knowledge on Phonetics and Chinese Characters

十

1. 汉字的偏旁（10） Radicals of Chinese characters (10)

偏旁 Radicals	例字 Examples	部件组合 Combinations	结构图示 Illustrations
穴	空	穴＋工	⊟
	突	穴＋犬	⊟
	穿	穴＋牙	⊟
田	男	田＋力	⊟
	累	田＋糸	⊟
	思	田＋心	⊟
	备	夂＋田	⊟
	留	卯＋田	⊟
力	加	力＋口	⊟
	动	云＋力	⊟
	努	奴＋力	⊟
牛	物	牛＋勿	⊟
	特	牛＋寺	⊟

2. 认读下列词语，并试着读写构成词语的汉字 Recognize the following words, and try to read and write the Chinese characters forming these words

tūrán　　tèbié　　jiāshí　　tíngliú
突然　　特别　　加时　　停留

| 突 | 然 | | | | | 特 | 别 | | | | |
| 加 | 时 | | | | | 停 | 留 | | | | |

29

2 Dǎoyóu zhuānyè zhīshi
导游专业知识
Tour Guide Expertise

项目一 Item 1
出入境知识与手续 Knowledge and Procedures for Exit and Entry

题解 Introduction

1. 学习内容：出入境的基本知识和出入境程序。
   Learning content: The basic knowledge and procedures for exit and entry.
2. 知识目标：掌握与接待旅游团入境有关的核心词语及表述。
   Knowledge objectives: To acquire the core words and expressions related to receiving inbound tourist groups.
3. 技能目标：能帮助游客正确填写入境卡和健康申报卡，顺利出入海关。
   Skill objective: To be able to fill in the entry card and health declaration card correctly and enter or exit customs successfully.

一、热身 rèshēn Warm-up

1. 给词语选择对应的图片。 Choose the corresponding pictures for the words.

A.

B.

C.

D.

❶ qiānzhèng
签证 _____
visa

❷ rùjìngkǎ
入境卡 _____
enrty card

❸ hùzhào
护照 _____
passport

❹ chūjìng shēnqǐngbiǎo
出境 申请表 _____
exit application form

2. 观看介绍出入境红色通道和绿色通道的视频，判断下列情况应该走哪个通道。
   Watch the video introducing the Red Channel GOODS TO DECLARE channel and the Green Channel NOTHING TO DECLARE channel, and tell which channel should be taken in the following situations.

A. 红色通道 hóngsè tōngdào
GOODS TO DECLARE

B. 绿色通道 lǜsè tōngdào
NOTHING TO DECLARE

① 李华行李里带了1条香烟。（　　）
   Li Hua has 1 carton of cigarettes in his luggage.

② 王东持有外交签证。（　　）
   Wang Dong has a diplomatic visa.

③ 张强行李里有单价超过5000元人民币的照相机。（　　）
   There are cameras with a unit price exceeding 5000 RMB in Zhang Qiang's luggage.

④ 赵云行李里有5根金条。（　　）
   Zhao Yun has five gold bars in his luggage.

⑤ 王方行李里有一瓶茅台酒。（　　）
   Wang Fang has a bottle of Maotai in his luggage.

❻ Lǐ Dān chíyǒu lǐyù qiānzhèng.（　　）
李丹持有礼遇签证。
Li Dan has a courtesy visa.

二、课文　kèwén　Texts

A 🎧 02-01

dǎoyóu: Huānyíng láidào Jiǎnpǔzhài, rùjìng qián qǐng nín tiánxiě rùjìngkǎ.
导游：欢迎来到柬埔寨，入境前请您填写入境卡。

yóukè: Hǎo de, wǒ kàn bu dǒng Jiǎnpǔzhàiyǔ hé Yīngyǔ, néng qǐng nín bāngmáng ma?
游客：好的，我看不懂柬埔寨语和英语，能请您帮忙吗？

dǎoyóu: Hǎo de, nín xiān zài zhèli tiánxiě xìngmíng, chūshēng dìdiǎn hé rìqī. Jiē xialai tiánxiě
导游：好的，您先在这里填写姓名、出生地点和日期。接下来填写

guójí, hùzhàohào, hángbānhào, láizì hé chù, qiānzhèng lèixíng, qiānfā dìdiǎn.
国籍、护照号、航班号、来自何处、签证类型、签发地点。

Zuìhòu tiánxiě rùjìng mùdì, tíngliú tiān shù hé zài Jiǎnpǔzhài jūzhù de dìzhǐ.
最后填写入境目的、停留天数和在柬埔寨居住的地址。

yóukè: Wǒ tiánhǎo le, hái yǒu shénme xūyào wǒ tiánxiě ma?
游客：我填好了，还有什么需要我填写吗？

dǎoyóu: Hǎiguān shēnbàobiǎo.
导游：海关申报表。

导游专业知识
Tour Guide Expertise 2

译文 yìwén Text in English

Tour Guide: Welcome to Cambodia. Please fill in the entry card before arrival.
Traveller: OK. I don't know Cambodian and English. Can you help me?
Tour Guide: Ok. Please fill in your name, place and date of birth here. Then, fill in your nationality, passport number, flight number, place of origin, visa type and place of issue. Finally, fill in the purpose of entry, length of stay and address of residence in Cambodia.
Traveller: I've filled it in. Is there anything else I need to fill in?
Tour Guide: Customs declaration form.

普通词语 pǔtōng cíyǔ General Vocabulary 🎧 02-02

1.	填写	tiánxiě	v.	fill in
2.	目的	mùdì	n.	purpose
3.	停留	tíngliú	v.	stay
4.	地址	dìzhǐ	n.	address

专业词语 zhuānyè cíyǔ Specialized Vocabulary 🎧 02-03

1.	导游	dǎoyóu	n.	tour guide
2.	国籍	guójí	n.	nationality
3.	护照号	hùzhàohào	n.	passport number
4.	航班号	hángbānhào	n.	flight number
5.	签证	qiānzhèng	n.	visa
6.	类型	lèixíng	n.	type
7.	签发	qiānfā	v.	issue
8.	海关申报表	hǎiguān shēnbàobiǎo	phr.	Customs Declaration Form

B 🎧 02-04

dǎoyóu: Nǐmen hǎo! Wǒ shì Xiǎo'ài, hěn róngxìng gěi nǐmen dāng dǎoyóu, zài Jiǎnpǔzhài de 6
导游：你们好！我是小爱，很荣幸给你们当导游，在柬埔寨的6
rì lǚyóu yóu wǒ wèi nǐmen ānpái xíngchéng.
日旅游由我为你们安排行程。

yóukè: Xiǎo'ài, nín hǎo! Xiànzài wǒmen shì qù jiǔdiàn ma?
游客：小爱，您好！现在我们是去酒店吗？

dǎoyóu: Shìde. Wǒmen jīnwǎn zhù Jīnbiān Dà Jiǔdiàn. Wèilái jǐ tiān wǒ jiāng dàilǐng nín cānguān
导游：是的。我们今晚住金边大酒店。未来几天我将带领您参观

Wúgē Kū, Jīnbiān Wánggōng, Dúlì Jìniànbēi, Zhōngxíng Tǎ hé Bīnjiāng Gōngyuán.
吴哥窟、金边 王宫、独立纪念碑、钟形 塔和 滨江 公园。

Qǐng gēn wǒ shàng chē.
请 跟我上 车。

yóukè: Qǐngwèn xūyào duō cháng shíjiān dào jiǔdiàn?
游客: 请问需要多 长 时间到酒店？

dǎoyóu: Dàgài 40 fēnzhōng. Nǐmen kěyǐ zài chē shang xiān xiūxi yíxiàr.
导游: 大概40分钟。你们 可以 在 车 上 先休息一下儿。

译文 yìwén Text in English

Tour Guide: Hello! I am Xiao Ai. It is my honor to be your guide. I will arrange your itinerary for your 6-day tour in Cambodia.

Traveller: Hello, Xiao Ai! Are we checking into a hotel now?

Tour Guide: Yes. We'll stay at Phnom Penh Hotel tonight. In the coming days I will take you to Angkor Wat, the Royal Palace in Phnom Penh, the Independence Monument, the Wat Phnom and the Riverside Park. Please follow me to the bus.

Traveller: How long will it take to get to the hotel?

Tour Guide: About 40 minutes. You can have a rest on the bus.

普通词语 pǔtōng cíyǔ General Vocabulary 🎧 02-05

1.	荣幸	róngxìng	adj.	honored
2.	带领	dàilǐng	v.	take (sb.) to (a place)
3.	行程	xíngchéng	n.	itinerary
4.	参观	cānguān	v.	visit
5.	跟	gēn	v.	follow
6.	休息	xiūxi	v.	rest

专业词语 zhuānyè cíyǔ Specialized Vocabulary 🎧 02-06

1.	吴哥窟	Wúgē Kū	pn.	Angkor Wat
2.	金边王宫	Jīnbiān Wánggōng	pn.	the Royal Palace of Phnom Penh
3.	独立纪念碑	Dúlì Jìniànbēi	pn.	the Independence Monument
4.	钟形塔	Zhōngxíng Tǎ	pn.	the Wat Phnom
5.	滨江公园	Bīnjiāng Gōngyuán	pn.	the Riverside Park

三、视听说　shì-tīng-shuō　Viewing, Listening, and Speaking

观看介绍安全检查内容的视频，将违禁物品的序号写在横线上，并说一说哪些物品属于违禁物品。
Watch the video introducing the content of the security check, write the number of prohibited items in the blank, and explain which items are considered prohibited.

qiāngzhī dànyào
① 枪支 弹药
arms and ammunition

xiāngyān
② 香烟
cigarettes

yì bào wùpǐn
③ 易爆物品
explosives

fǔshí wùpǐn
④ 腐蚀物品
corrosives

bái jiǔ
⑤ 白酒
liquor

yǒu dú wùpǐn
⑥ 有毒物品
toxic substances

fàngshèxìng wùpǐn
⑦ 放射性 物品
radioactive substances

yàopǐn
⑧ 药品
drug

违禁物品：_____
prohibited items

说一说　Let's talk

说出哪些物品属于违禁品。　Practice saying which items are considered prohibited.

四、学以致用 xuéyǐzhìyòng Practicing What You Have Learnt

听录音，了解入境柬埔寨的程序，将下列入境步骤排序。

Listen to the recording to learn the procedures for entering Cambodia and arrange the following steps in order.

A. Tiánxiě liǎng zhāng Jiǎnpǔzhài hǎiguān tígōng de rùjìng dēngjìbiǎo, bāokuò rùjìng yímínkǎ, hǎiguān shēnbàobiǎo.
填写 两 张 柬埔寨 海关 提供 的 入境 登记表，包括 入境 移民卡、海关 申报表。

Fill in two entry registration forms provided by the Cambodian Customs, including the immigration card and the customs declaration form.

 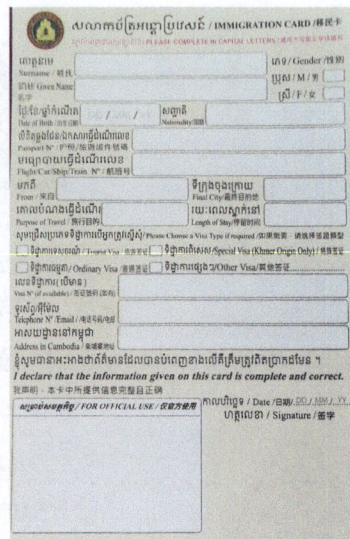 

B. Tíqǔ hángyùn xíngli.
提取 航运 行李。

Claim checked baggage.

C. Rú xū bàn luòdìqiān, dàodá jīchǎng hòu, qiánwǎng bànlǐ qiānzhèng chuāngkǒu bànlǐ, rú yǐjīng bànlǐ qiānzhèng, dào rùjìngchù bànlǐ chūguān.
如需办 落地签，到达 机场 后，前往 办理 签证 窗口 办理，如已经办理 签证，到 入境处 办理 出关。

If you need to apply for a visa on arrival, go to the visa processing window after arriving at the airport. If you already have a visa, go to the immigration counter for clearance.

D. Zhǔnbèi hùzhào、qiānzhèng hé měiyuán xiànjīn.
准备 护照、签证 和美元 现金。

Prepare your passport, visa, and US Dollar cash.

① _____   ② _____   ③ _____   ④ _____

五、小知识　xiǎo zhīshi　Tips

Chūjìng xiǎo zhīshi
出境 小知识

　　Gēnjù Zhōngguó hǎiguān guīdìng, měi rén měi cì chūjìng kě xiédài xiànjīn bù néng chāoguò 20000 yuán rénmínbì huò 5000 měijīn huò 35000 gǎngbì huò děngzhí yú shàngshù huòbì.
根据中国海关规定，每人每次出境可携带现金不能超过20000元人民币或5000美金或35000港币或等值于上述货币。

　　Rùjìng shí měi rén kě miǎnshuì xiédài dàyuē 1 píng jiǔ、2 tiáo xiāngyān. Gāojí zhàoxiàngjī、shèxiàngjī、shǒutí diànnǎo děng wùpǐn xūyào zài hǎiguān shēnbào, sānjiǎojià yào tuōyùn. Jìnzhǐ xiédài rùjìng de wùpǐn bāokuò dúpǐn、wǔqì、mázuìxìng yàowù、jìngwài shuǐguǒ、gǔdǒng děng děng.
入境时每人可免税携带大约1瓶酒、2条香烟。高级照相机、摄像机、手提电脑等物品需要在海关申报，三角架要托运。禁止携带入境的物品包括毒品、武器、麻醉性药物、境外水果、古董等等。

Exit Trip Tips

According to Chinese customs regulations, each person can take no more than 20,000 yuan, 5,000 US dollars, 35,000 HK dollars, or the equivalent in other currencies per trip.

Each person is allowed to bring in approximately one bottle of wine and two cartons of cigarettes duty-free upon entry. High-end cameras, camcorders, laptops and similar items need to be declared at customs, while tripods must be checked in. Prohibited items include drugs, weapons, narcotic drugs, foreign fruits, antiques and so on.

项目小结 Item Summary

cíyǔ 词语 Vocabulary

普通词语 General Vocabulary

1.	填写	tiánxiě	v.	fill in
2.	目的	mùdì	n.	purpose
3.	停留	tíngliú	v.	stay
4.	地址	dìzhǐ	n.	address
5.	荣幸	róngxìng	adj.	honored
6.	带领	dàilǐng	v.	take (sb.) to (a place)
7.	行程	xíngchéng	n.	itinerary
8.	参观	cānguān	v.	visit
9.	跟	gēn	v.	follow
10.	休息	xiūxi	v.	rest

专业词语 Specialized Vocabulary

1.	导游	dǎoyóu	n.	tour guide
2.	国籍	guójí	n.	nationality
3.	护照号	hùzhàohào	n.	passport number
4.	航班号	hángbānhào	n.	flight number
5.	签证	qiānzhèng	n.	visa
6.	类型	lèixíng	n.	type
7.	签发	qiānfā	v.	issue
8.	海关申报表	hǎiguān shēnbàobiǎo	phr.	Customs Declaration Form
9.	吴哥窟	Wúgē Kū	pn.	Angkor Wat
10.	金边王宫	Jīnbiān Wánggōng	pn.	the Royal Palace of Phnom Penh
11.	独立纪念碑	Dúlì Jìniànbēi	pn.	the Independence Monument
12.	钟形塔	Zhōngxíng Tǎ	pn.	the Wat Phnom
13.	滨江公园	Bīnjiāng Gōngyuán	pn.	the Riverside Park

jùzi 句子 Sentences	1. 红色通道也称"应税通道"。 2. 绿色通道亦称"免税通道"或"无申报通道"。 3. 安全检查的内容主要是检查旅客及其行李物品中是否携带枪支、弹药，易爆、腐蚀、有毒、放射性等危险物品。 4. 您先在这里填写姓名、出生地点和日期。接下来填写国籍、护照号、航班号、来自何处、签证类型、签发地点。最后填写入境目的，停留天数和在柬埔寨居住的地址。

项目二 Item 2
旅游安全知识 Knowledge on Travel Safety

题解 Introduction

1. 学习内容：旅游时的交通、住宿、游览和饮食安全知识。
   Learning content: The knowledge of transportation, accommodation, sightseeing and food safety during travelling.
2. 知识目标：掌握与带团旅游时安全提醒有关的核心词语及表述。
   Knowledge objectives: To acquire core words and expressions related to safety reminders when leading group tours.
3. 技能目标：帮助游客避免和处理旅行中的安全问题。
   Skill objective: To be able to help tourists avoid and deal with safety problems during traveling.

一、热身 rèshēn Warm-up

1. 给词语选择对应的图片。Choose the corresponding pictures for the words.

A.　　　　　　　B.　　　　　　　C.　　　　　　　D.

① jìnzhǐ pāizhào
禁止拍照 _____
No photography

② yánjìn yānhuǒ
严禁烟火 _____
No open flames

③ jíjiùzhàn
急救站 _____
First aid station

④ jǐnjí chūkǒu
紧急出口 _____
Emergency exit

2. 看视频，了解旅行中的安全知识，并将安全知识归入对应的类别。
   Watch the video to learn knowledge on travel safety, and classify the safety knowledge into the corresponding categories.

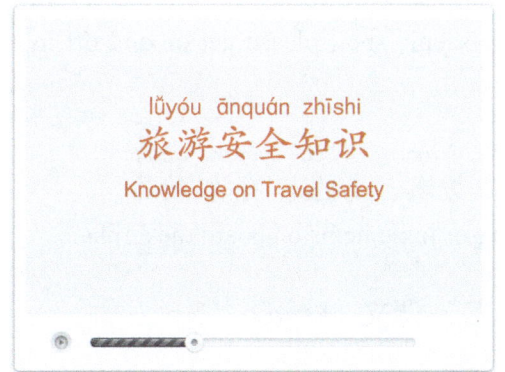

lǚyóu ānquán zhīshi
旅游安全知识
Knowledge on Travel Safety

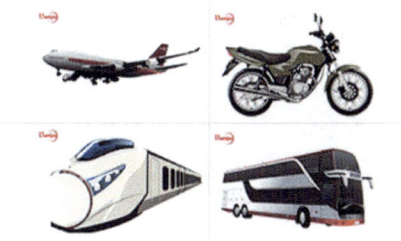

① jiāotōng gōngjù ānquán
交通 工具 安全
safety of means of transportation
_____

② jǐngqū yóulǎn ānquán
景区 游览 安全
tourist safety at scenic spots
_____

③ gòuwù yǐnshí ānquán
购物饮食安全
safety of shopping and eating
_____

④ jiǔdiàn zhùsù ānquán
酒店 住宿安全
safety of hotel accommodation
_____

A. Chūrù jiǔdiàn fángjiān qǐng suíshǒu guānmén, wù jiāng yīwù pī zài dēng shang huò zài chuáng shang chōuyān.
出入酒店房间请随手关门，勿将衣物披在灯上或在床上抽烟。
Close the door behind you when entering and leaving the hotel room. Do not put clothes on the lamp or smoke in bed.

B. Bù suíyì gòumǎi、shíyòng jiētóu xiǎotānfàn de lièzhì shípǐn、yǐnliào.
不随意购买、食用街头小摊贩的劣质食品、饮料。
Do not buy or eat low-quality food and beverages from street vendors.

C. Jǐngqū dāchéng lǎnchē shí, qǐng yī xù shàngxià, tīngcóng gōngzuò rényuán zhǐhuī.
景区搭乘缆车时，请依序上下，听从工作人员指挥。
When taking the cable car at the scenic spot, please get on and off in order, and follow the staff's guidance.

D. Chéngzuò fēijī shí bù néng xiédài yì rán、yì bào、yǒu dú wùpǐn.
乘坐飞机时不能携带易燃、易爆、有毒物品。
Do not carry flammable, explosive or toxic items on board the airplane.

二、课文 kèwén Texts

A 03-01

dǎoyóu: Huānyíng dàjiā láidào Jiǎnpǔzhài. Jiē xialai jǐ tiān de lǚxíng zhōng, wǒmen xūyāo chéngzuò fēijī、dàbā hé lúnchuán děng jiāotōng gōngjù.
导游：欢迎大家来到柬埔寨。接下来几天的旅行中，我们需要乘坐飞机、大巴和轮船等交通工具。

yóukè: Wǒmen yào zhùyì nǎxiē ānquán shìxiàng ne?
游客：我们要注意哪些安全事项呢？

dǎoyóu: Dāchéng fēijī shí, dàjiā yào jìhǎo ānquándài, bú dài wēixiǎnpǐn huò yìránpǐn. Chéngjī. Fēijī shēngjiàng qījiān, búyào shǐyòng shǒujī děng diànzǐ chǎnpǐn. Chéngzuò dàbā shí búyào jiāng tóu、shǒu shēnchū chuāng wài, shàngxià chē shí zhùyì guānchá zhōuwéi qíngkuàng. Dāchéng yóulún shí, búyào zài chuánshang pǎotiào、dǎnào, yào láojì jiùshēngyī、jiùshēngchuán、mièhuǒqì de wèizhì jí shǐyòng fāngfǎ.
导游：搭乘飞机时，大家要系好安全带，不带危险品或易燃品。乘机。飞机升降期间，不要使用手机等电子产品。乘坐大巴时不要将头、手伸出窗外，上下车时注意观察周围情况。搭乘游轮时，不要在船上跑跳、打闹，要牢记救生衣、救生船、灭火器的位置及使用方法。

yóukè: Xièxie nín gàosu wǒmen zhèxiē jiāotōng ānquán zhīshi.
游客：谢谢您告诉我们这些交通安全知识。

导游专业知识
Tour Guide Expertise 2

译文 yìwén Text in English

Tour Guide: Welcome to Cambodia. During the next few days, we will travel by plane, bus and ship.

Traveller: What safety precautions should we pay attention to?

Tour Guide: When taking a plane, fasten your seat belts, and do not carry inflammable materials or dangerous articles. Do not use mobile phones or electronic products when the plane takes off and lands. Don't put your head and hands out of the window when taking a bus. Watch out when getting on and off the bus. When taking a cruise ship, do not run or jump aboard. Keep in mind the location and usage of life jackets, lifeboats, and fire extinguishers.

Traveller: Thank you for sharing these traffic safety tips.

普通词语 pǔtōng cíyǔ General Vocabulary   03-02

1.	旅行	lǚxíng	v.	travel
2.	轮船	lúnchuán	n.	ship
3.	注意	zhùyì	v.	pay attention to
4.	危险	wēixiǎn	adj.	dangerous
5.	观察	guānchá	v.	observe
6.	牢记	láojì	v.	keep in mind

专业词语 zhuānyè cíyǔ Specialized Vocabulary   03-03

1.	交通工具	jiāotōng gōngjù	phr.	means of transportation
2.	搭乘	dāchéng	v.	travel by
3.	安全带	ānquándài	n.	seat belt
4.	易燃品	yìránpǐn	n.	inflammable material
5.	游轮	yóulún	n.	cruise ship
6.	救生衣	jiùshēngyī	n.	life jacket
7.	救生船	jiùshēngchuán	n.	lifeboat
8.	灭火器	mièhuǒqì	n.	fire extinguisher

B 🎧 03-04

导游： 我们马上就到今天游览的景点金边王宫了。

游客： 景区游览有哪些安全注意事项呢？

导游： 首先，大家要记住我们的集合地点、时间、所乘游览巴士的车牌号。另外，要注意饮食安全，不要购买无证摊贩出售的食品。如果游客比较多，大家不要拥堵在入口处，请按照工作人员的指引排队，有序进入。进入景区后，注意查看景区设施上的安全标志，严禁在景区抽烟。保管好您的贵重物品。

游客： 谢谢您的提醒。

译文 yìwén Text in English

Tour Guide: We are approaching our destination: the Royal Palace in Phnom Penh.

Traveller: What are the safety precautions for visiting a scenic spot?

Tour Guide: First, we should remember our gathering place and time, and the license number of our tour bus. In addition, pay attention to food safety, and do not buy food from unlicensed vendors. If there are many tourists, do not crowd at the entrance, and queue up following the staff's instructions for orderly entry. Pay attention to safety signs on the facilities in the scenic spot. It is strictly prohibited to smoke in the scenic spot. Keep your valuables safe.

Traveller: Thanks for your tips.

普通词语 pǔtōng cíyǔ General Vocabulary 🎧 03-05

1.	景区	jǐngqū	n.	scenic spot
2.	集合	jíhé	v.	gather
3.	出售	chūshòu	v.	sell
4.	拥堵	yōngdǔ	v.	crowd
5.	贵重	guìzhòng	adj.	precious

专业词语 zhuānyè cíyǔ Specialized Vocabulary 🎧 03-06

1.	游览	yóulǎn	v.	go sightseeing
2.	车牌号	chēpáihào	n.	license plate number
3.	饮食安全	yǐnshí ānquán	phr.	food safety
4.	无证摊贩	wúzhèng tānfàn	phr.	unlicensed vendor
5.	设施	shèshī	n.	facility
6.	标志	biāozhì	n.	sign
7.	严禁	yánjìn	v.	strictly prohibit
8.	保管	bǎoguǎn	v.	take care of

三、视听说　shì-tīng-shuō　Viewing, Listening, and Speaking

看视频，了解安全注意事项，请在不安全的项目下打上 ×，并说出正确的处置方法。

Watch the video to learn about safety precautions, mark the unsafe items with an "×" and describe the correct handling method.

① wàichū shí xiédài dàliàng xiànjīn
外出时携带大量现金 _____

Carry a lot of cash when you are out.

② cānjiā shuǐshang huódòng, àn guīdìng chuānzhuó jiùshēngyī
参加水上活动，按规定穿着救生衣
_____

Wear life jackets in water sports as required.

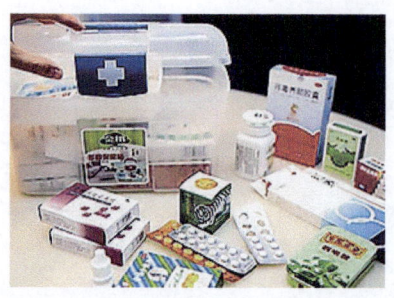

③ lǚxíng zhōng dài yìxiē bìbèi de yàopǐn
旅行中带一些必备的药品
_____

Bring with you some essential medicines during your trip.

④ chéng chuán shí, bú zài chuántóu、jiǎbǎn děng dì zhuīzhú、dǎnào
乘船时，不在船头、甲板等地
追逐、打闹 _____

Do not horse around in the bow, on the deck, etc. when taking a boat ride.

⑤ jiǔdiàn zhùsù shí, tīngdào huǒjǐnglíng xiǎng, lìkè dāchéng diàntī xià lóu
酒店住宿时，听到火警铃响，
立刻搭乘电梯下楼 _____

Take the elevator downstairs immediately in the case of a fire alarm in the hotel.

⑥ dāchéng lǎnchē shí, zìxíng dǎkāi jiàoxiāngmén huò hùlán
搭乘缆车时，自行打开轿厢门或
护栏 _____

Open the car door or guardrail by yourself when taking a cable car.

说一说　Let's talk

说一说你所知道的旅行安全知识。　Talk about the travel safety tips you know.

四、学以致用　xuéyǐzhìyòng　Practicing What We Have Learnt

看视频，了解导游带领游客游览景区时的程序，将下列步骤排序。
Watch the video to learn the procedures for a tour guide to show tourists around a scenic spot, and sequence the steps below.

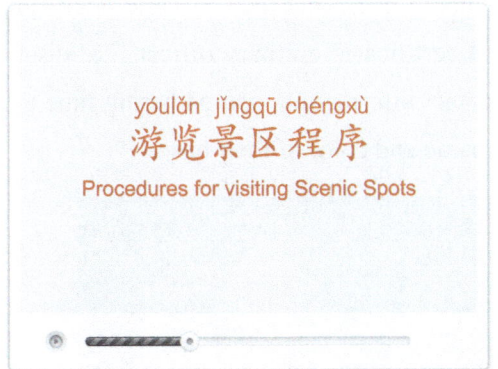

A. Dàodá jǐngqū hòu, ànzhào xiéyìjià gòumǎi ménpiào, rú yù értóngjià bù hán jǐngdiǎn ménpiào、lǎnchē xū
到达景区后，按照协议价购买门票，如遇儿童价不含景点门票、缆车需éwài shōufèi děng wèntí, tíqián yǔ yóukè gōutōng, xiézhù yóukè bànlǐ piàowù děng shǒuxù.
额外收费等问题，提前与游客沟通，协助游客办理票务等手续。

Upon arrival, purchase the tickets at the negotiated price. If the children's price does not include the scenic spot tickets or the cable car is charged additionally, communicate with the tourists with advance and assist them with ticketing and other procedures.

B. 前往景区前，提醒游客贵重物品随身携带。提醒有门票优惠的游客，携带并出示学生证、老年证、离退休证、军官证、残疾证等有效证件。告知游客导游的联系方式、集合时间和地点，提醒游客记清所乘大巴的车牌号码、车辆名称和颜色特征。

Before heading for the scenic spot, remind tourists to keep their valuables with them. Remind tourists who are eligible for ticket discounts to bring and present valid documents such as student ID cards, senior citizen ID cards, retirement certificates, military officer IDs, disability certificates, etc. Inform the tourists of the tour guide's contact information, and gathering time and place. Remind the tourists to remember the license number, name and color of their bus.

C. 游玩结束后，查点和确认游客人数。发车前往用餐酒店前，提前联系和安排好游客的用餐。

After the tour, check and confirm the number of tourists. Before leaving for the hotel, contact and arrange the meal for the tourists in advance.

D. 在景区游玩时，提醒游客注意安全。做好景点的讲解工作，合理安排游客拍照留念和休息的时间。提醒游客集合时间和地点。

When visiting the scenic spot, remind the tourists to pay attention to safety. Interpret the scenic spot conscientiously, arrange time for tourists to take pictures and rest reasonably, and remind the tourists of the gathering time and place.

① _____ ② _____ ③ _____ ④ _____

五、小知识 xiǎo zhīshi Tips

游客住宿安全知识
Yóukè zhùsù ānquán zhīshi

导游要清楚客人所住房间的楼层、位置及房间号,熟悉值班室和酒店的安全紧急通道。一旦发生危险情况,能组织客人迅速、安全地撤离现场,避免伤亡。提醒客人出门时携带好自己的房间钥匙,贵重物品随身保管或寄存。提醒楼层服务员,不要贸然给未持钥匙但要进入自己或他人房间的客人开门。提醒客人睡前关好窗户,搭上门扣,不要给陌生人开门。

导游应将自己的房间号及联系方式告知客人和酒店负责人。如给客人打电话,请先自报家门。

Tips on Tourists' Accommodation Safety

The tour guide should know the floor, location and room number of each guest, and be familiar with the duty room and the emergency exit of the hotel. In the case of an emergency, the guide can evacuate the guests quickly and safely to avoid casualties. The guide should remind guests to bring their room keys when going out, and to either take care of or deposit their valuables. The guide should remind the floor attendant not to open the door rashly for guests attempting to enter their own room or another guest's room without a key. The guide should remind guests to close the windows and secure the door latch before going to bed, and not to open the door for strangers. The tour guide should inform the guests and the person in charge of the hotel of his/her room number and contact information. When calling a guest, the guide should introduce himself/herself first.

项目小结 Item Summary

词语 cíyǔ Vocabulary

普通词语　General Vocabulary

1.	旅行	lǚxíng	v.	travel
2.	轮船	lúnchuán	n.	ship
3.	注意	zhùyì	v.	pay attention to
4.	危险	wēixiǎn	adj.	dangerous
5.	观察	guānchá	v.	observe
6.	牢记	láojì	v.	keep in mind
7.	景区	jǐngqū	n.	scenic spot
8.	集合	jíhé	v.	gather
9.	出售	chūshòu	v.	sell
10.	拥堵	yōngdǔ	v.	crowd
11.	贵重	guìzhòng	adj.	precious

专业词语　Specialized Vocabulary

1.	交通工具	jiāotōng gōngjù	phr.	means of transportation
2.	搭乘	dāchéng	v.	travel by
3.	安全带	ānquándài	n.	seat belt
4.	易燃品	yìránpǐn	n.	inflammable material
5.	游轮	yóulún	n.	cruise ship
6.	救生衣	jiùshēngyī	n.	life jacket
7.	救生船	jiùshēngchuán	n.	lifeboat
8.	灭火器	mièhuǒqì	n.	fire extinguisher
9.	游览	yóulǎn	v.	go sightseeing
10.	车牌号	chēpáihào	n.	license plate number
11.	饮食安全	yǐnshí ānquán	phr.	food safety
12.	无证摊贩	wúzhèng tānfàn	n.	unlicensed vendors
13.	设施	shèshī	n.	facility
14.	标志	biāozhì	n.	sign
15.	严禁	yánjìn	v.	strictly prohibit
16.	保管	bǎoguǎn	v.	take care of

句子 jùzi Sentences

1. 搭乘飞机时，大家要系好安全带，不带危险品或易燃品乘机。
2. 乘坐大巴时不要将头、手伸出窗外。
3. 要牢记救生衣、救生船、灭火器的位置及使用方法。
4. 要注意饮食安全，不要购买无证摊贩出售的食品。
5. 注意查看景区设施上的安全标志，严禁在景区抽烟。

项目三 Item 3

通信知识 Knowledge on Communication

题解 Introduction

1. 学习内容：境外通信的基本知识和通信种类的选择。
   Learning content: The basic knowledge of overseas communication and the choice of communication types.
2. 知识目标：掌握与帮助旅游团选择和比较不同通信方式有关的核心词语及表述。
   Knowledge objectives: To acquire the core words and expressions related to helping tour groups choose and compare different communication ways.
3. 技能目标：能帮助旅游团选择合适的通信方式和资费套餐。
   Skill objective: To be able to help the tour group choose the appropriate communication way and price packet service.

一、热身　rèshēn　Warm-up

1. 给词语选择对应的图片。　Choose the corresponding pictures for the words.

　A.　　　　　　　　B.　　　　　　　　C.　　　　　　　　D.

中文 + 景点导游

① tōngxìn shèbèi
  通信 设备 _____
  communication equipment

② yídòng WIFI
  移动 WIFI _____
  portable WiFi

③ yùnyíngshāng
  运营商 _____
  operator

④ SIM kǎ
  SIM 卡 _____
  SIM card

2. 看视频，了解柬埔寨的三大电信运营商，并与其所属国家连线。
Watch the video to learn about the three telecom operators in Cambodia, and match them with their countries.

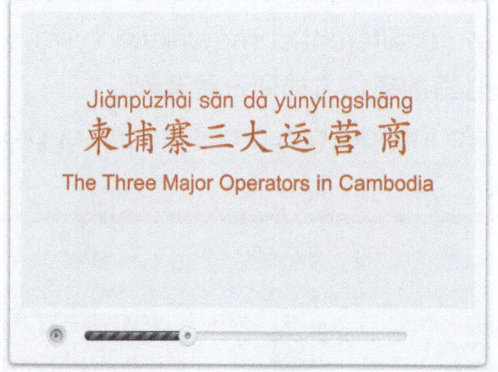

Jiǎnpǔzhài sān dà yùnyíngshāng
柬埔寨三大运营商
The Three Major Operators in Cambodia

Mǎláixīyà
马来西亚
Malaysia

Jiǎnpǔzhài
柬埔寨
Cambodia

Yuènán
越南
Vietnam

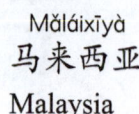

二、课文 kèwén Texts

A 🎧 04-01

dǎoyóu: Huānyíng nín dǐdá Jīnbiān Guójì Jīchǎng, lǚchéng xīnkǔ le.
导游：欢迎您抵达金边国际机场，旅程辛苦了。

yóukè: Xièxie, néng qǐng nín bāngmáng bànlǐ yì zhāng Jiǎnpǔzhài de shǒujīkǎ ma?
游客：谢谢，能请您帮忙办理一张柬埔寨的手机卡吗？

dǎoyóu: Hǎo de, qǐng gēn wǒ lái. Běn jīchǎng yǒu sān jiā yùnyíngshāng kě gōng xuǎnzé,
导游：好的，请跟我来。本机场有三家运营商可供选择，

Smart、Cellcard hé Metfone.
Smart、Cellcard 和 Metfone。

yóukè: Wǒ xuǎn Cellcard, jiē xialai zěnme zuò?
游客：我选 Cellcard，接下来怎么做？

dǎoyóu: Qǐng chūshì nín de hùzhào gěi gōngzuò rényuán, bìng xuǎnzé liúliàng tàocān.
导游：请出示您的护照给工作人员，并选择流量套餐。

yóukè: Hǎo de, ránhòu ne?
游客：好的，然后呢？

dǎoyóu: Qǐng xuǎnzé nín xūyào chōngzhí de jīn'é, shì shuākǎ háishi fù xiànjīn?
导游：请选择您需要充值的金额，是刷卡还是付现金？

yóukè: Fù xiànjīn, xièxie.
游客：付现金，谢谢。

dǎoyóu: Chōngzhí wánchéng le, zhè shì nín Jiǎnpǔzhài de SIM kǎ, chā zài shǒujī li
导游：充值完成了，这是您柬埔寨的SIM卡，插在手机里

jiù kěyǐ shǐyòng le.
就可以使用了。

译文 yìwén Text in English

Tour Guide: Welcome to Phnom Penh International Airport. You must be tired from the journey.

Traveller: Thank you. Can you help me get a Cambodian mobile phone card?

Tour Guide: OK. Please follow me. There are three operators to choose from: Smart, Cellcard and Metfone.

Traveller: I choose Cellcard. What should I do next?

Tour Guide: Please show your passport to the staff and choose the data package.

Traveller: OK, then what?

Tour Guide: Please choose the recharge amount. Would you like to pay by credit card or in cash?

Traveller: In cash, thank you.

Tour Guide: The recharge is completed. This is your SIM card in Cambodia. You can use your phone after inserting the card into your mobile phone.

普通词语 pǔtōng cíyǔ General Vocabulary 🎧 04-02

1.	抵达	dǐdá	v.	arrive
2.	旅程	lǚchéng	n.	journey
3.	出示	chūshì	v.	show
4.	金额	jīn'é	n.	amount of money
5.	刷卡	shuākǎ	v.	pay by card
6.	现金	xiànjīn	n.	cash

专业词语 zhuānyè cíyǔ Specialized Vocabulary 🎧 04-03

1.	运营商	yùnyíngshāng	n.	operator
2.	流量	liúliàng	n.	data
3.	套餐	tàocān	n.	package
4.	充值	chōngzhí	v.	recharge

B 🎧 04-04

导游: 你们好！我是小爱，很荣幸给你们当导游，大家的手机都可以正常使用了吗？

游客: 小爱，您好！我不想买柬埔寨当地的 SIM 卡，有没有其他方式可以上网？

导游: 有。您还可以租用便携的 WIFI 设备，也是可以上网的。

游客: 请问机场有租赁点吗？是什么价格？

导游: 有，请跟我来。便携 WIFI 的租金是单价乘行程天数乘台数加押金。

游客: 好的，我需要一台。

导游专业知识 2
Tour Guide Expertise

译文 yìwén Text in English

Tour Guide: Hello! I'm Xiao Ai. I'm honored to be your tour guide. Can your mobile phones be used normally?

Traveller: Hello, Xiao Ai! I don't want to buy a local SIM card in Cambodia. Is there any other way to surf the Internet?

Tour Guide: Yes. You can rent a portable WiFi device to surf the Internet.

Traveller: Is there a rental point at the airport? What's the price?

Tour Guide: Yes, please follow me. The rent of a portable WiFi is unit price x days of your travel x number of sets + deposit.

Traveller: OK. I need one.

普通词语 pǔtōng cíyǔ General Vocabulary 🎧 04-05

1.	正常	zhèngcháng	adj.	normal
2.	使用	shǐyòng	v.	use
3.	其他	qítā	pron.	other
4.	方式	fāngshì	n.	way
5.	价格	jiàgé	n.	price

专业词语 zhuānyè cíyǔ Specialized Vocabulary 🎧 04-06

1.	上网	shàng//wǎng	v.	surf the Internet
2.	租用	zūyòng	v.	rent
3.	便携	biànxié	adj.	portable
4.	设备	shèbèi	n.	equipment
5.	租赁点	zūlìndiǎn	n.	rental point
6.	单价	dānjià	n.	unit price
7.	行程天数	xíngchéng tiān shù	phr.	days of (one's) travel
8.	押金	yājīn	n.	deposit

三、视听说　shì-tīng-shuō　Viewing, Listening, and Speaking

看视频，了解电话卡和便携 WIFI 的优缺点，判断下列描述是否正确。
Watch the video to learn the advantages and disadvantages of a telephone card and portable WiFi, and tell whether the following statements are true or false.

　　Gòumǎi dāngdì　SIM　kǎ de yōudiǎn shì xìnhào gèng wěndìng.
❶ 购买当地 SIM 卡的优点是信号更稳定。＿＿＿＿＿＿＿＿
　　The advantage of purchasing a local SIM card is its more stable signal.

　　Biànxié WIFI　zhǐ néng yì rén shǐyòng.
❷ 便携 WIFI 只能一人使用。＿＿＿＿＿＿＿＿
　　The portable WiFi can only be used by one person.

　　Dāngdì SIM　kǎ xūyào zhīfù　yídìng　jīn'é de yājīn.
❸ 当地 SIM 卡需要支付一定金额的押金。＿＿＿＿＿＿＿＿
　　A certain amount of deposit needs to be paid for a local SIM card.

　　Dāngdì SIM　kǎ zài yòngwán zhīhòu　xūyào guīhuán.
❹ 当地 SIM 卡在用完之后需要归还。＿＿＿＿＿＿＿＿
　　The local SIM card needs to be returned after use.

　　Biànxié　WIFI　xūyào chōngdiàn,　fǒuzé huì　wúfǎ shǐyòng.
❺ 便携 WIFI 需要充电，否则会无法使用。＿＿＿＿＿＿＿＿
　　The portable WiFi needs to be charged, otherwise it will not work.

说一说　Let's talk

说一说电话卡和便携 WIFI 的优缺点。
List the advantages and disadvantages of a telephone card and portable WiFi.

四、学以致用　xuéyǐzhìyòng　Practicing What You Have Learnt

听录音，了解柬埔寨酒店 WIFI 的使用政策，并指导游客在酒店连接网络。
Listen and learn the use policy of WiFi in Cambodian hotels, and instruct tourists to connect to the Internet in the hotel.

导游：尊敬的客人，您好！今晚我们将要入住的是位于金边的柬埔寨×××酒店，酒店为您提供了全程免费__❶__，您可以时刻与好友保持联系。信号覆盖酒店__❷__、__❸__、__❹__、__❺__等公共区域以及客房，您可以在酒店的任何位置畅快地使用 WIFI 网络。入住的客人使用手机打开 WIFI 上网功能，连接名为"Cambodian XXX Hotel"的 WIFI 信号，并在跳转页面中输入__❻__和办理入住的房客姓名，即可使用互联网了。

Tour Guide: Hello, dear guests! We are staying in Cambodia ××× Hotel in Phnom Penh tonight. The hotel provides you with free ___①___, so that you can always keep in touch with your friends. The signal covers hotel ___②___, ___③___, ___④___, ___⑤___ and other public areas and guest rooms, so you can use WiFi network freely in any place of the hotel. After check-in, turn on the WiFi Internet function, connect to the WiFi signal named "Cambodian XXX Hotel", enter the ___⑥___ and your name in the link page, and then you can use the Internet.

cāntīng
A. 餐厅
restaurant

fánghào
B. 房号
room number

dàtáng
C. 大堂
lobby

xíngzhèng jiǔláng
D. 行政 酒廊
executive lounge

WIFI fúwù
E. WIFI 服务
WIFI service

yǒngchí
F. 泳池
swimming pool

① _____   ② _____   ③ _____
④ _____   ⑤ _____   ⑥ _____

五、小知识 xiǎo zhīshi Tips

Guójì mànyóu zīfèi
国际漫游资费

Guójì mànyóu zīfèi shì yóu mànyóudì yùnyíngshāng guīdìng de, gègè yùnyíngshāng
国际 漫游 资费 是 由 漫游地 运营商 规定 的，各个 运营商
guīdìng de zīfèi biāozhǔn bù tóng. Zài chūguó zhīqián, guónèi de péngyou yě kěyǐ tōngguò
规定 的 资费 标准 不 同。在 出国 之前，国内 的 朋友 也 可以 通过
yùnyíngshāng de wǎngzhàn lái cháxún bùfen mànyóu zīfèi biāozhǔn. Dànshì yóuyú jìngwài
运营商 的 网站 来 查询 部分 漫游 资费 标准。但是 由于 境外

yùnyíngshāng zīfèi biāozhǔn yǒushí huì chūxiàn biànhuà, wàibì duìhuànlǜ yě suíshí huì biàngēng,
运营商 资费 标准 有时 会 出现 变化，外币 兑换率 也 随时 会 变更，

suǒyǐ zuìhǎo shì dào dāngdì hòu zài xiàng běndì yùnyíngshāng zīxún yí cì.
所以 最好 是 到 当地 后 再 向 本地 运营商 咨询 一 次。

International Roaming Charges

The international roaming charges are decided by the roaming destination's operators, and the charges vary among different operators. Before going abroad, you can check some roaming charges through the websites of operators. However, since the charges of overseas operators sometimes change and the foreign exchange rates fluctuate at any time, you'd better confirm the charges with the local operator again after your arrival.

项目小结 Item Summary

cíyǔ 词语 Vocabulary

普通词语 General Vocabulary

1.	抵达	dǐdá	v.	arrive
2.	旅程	lǚchéng	n.	journey
3.	出示	chūshì	v.	show
4.	金额	jīn'é	n.	amount of money
5.	刷卡	shuākǎ	v.	pay by card
6.	现金	xiànjīn	n.	cash
7.	正常	zhèngcháng	adj.	normal
8.	使用	shǐyòng	v.	use
9.	其他	qítā	adj.	other
10.	方式	fāngshì	n.	way
11.	价格	jiàgé	n.	price

专业词语 Specialized Vocabulary

1.	运营商	yùnyíngshāng	n.	operator
2.	流量	liúliàng	n.	data
3.	套餐	tàocān	n.	package
4.	充值	chōngzhí	v.	recharge
5.	上网	shàngwǎng	v.	surf the Internet
6.	租用	zūyòng	v.	rent
7.	便携	biànxié	adj.	portable
8.	设备	shèbèi	n.	equipment

		cíyǔ 词语 Vocabulary	9.	租赁点	zūlìndiǎn	n.	rental point
			10.	单价	dānjià	n.	unit price
			11.	行程天数	xíngchéng tiān shù	phr.	days of (one's) travel
			12.	押金	yājīn	n.	deposit

jùzi 句子 Sentences	1. 请出示您的护照给工作人员，并选择流量套餐。 2. 我不想买柬埔寨当地的SIM卡，有没有其他方式可以上网？ 3. 您还可以租用便携的WIFI设备，也是可以上网的。 4. 便携WIFI的租金是单价乘行程天数乘台数加押金。

项目四　Item 4
货币和保险知识　Knowledge on Currency and Insurance

题解　Introduction

1. 学习内容：货币和保险的基本知识。
   Learning content: The basic knowledge of currency and insurance.
2. 知识目标：掌握与进行索赔时的语言沟通有关的核心词语及表述。
   Knowledge objectives: To acquire the core words and expressions related to language communication for making claims.
3. 技能目标：能顺利完成出境前的货币准备和保险购买工作，熟悉索赔流程和保险单填写。
   Skill objective: To be able to complete currency preparation and insurance purchase before departure, and get familiar with claim process and insurance policy filling.

一、热身　rèshēn　Warm-up

1. 给词语选择对应的图片。　Choose the corresponding pictures for the words.

A.

B.

C.

D.

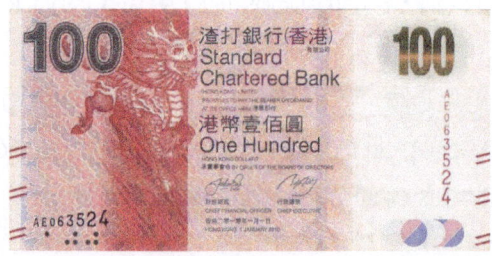

E.

F.

① měiyuán
美元 _____
USD

② rénmínbì
人民币 _____
RMB

③ gǎngbì
港币 _____
HKD

④ yuènándùn
越南盾 _____
VND

⑤ lǚxíng zhīpiào
旅行 支票 _____
traveler's check

⑥ xìnyòngkǎ
信用卡 _____
credit card

2. 看视频，了解出境游保险相关知识，判断下列情况可否进行索赔。
   Watch the video to learn about outbound travel insurance and determine if you can make a claim in each of the following cases.

chóng yǎo
A. 虫咬
Insect bite

sǐwáng
B. 死亡
Death

xíngli bèi dào
C. 行李被盗
Luggage is stolen

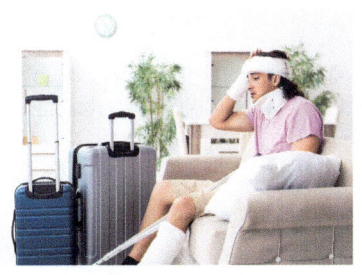

shòushāng
D. 受伤
Injury

可以进行索赔的是：_____
Cases where you can make a claim:

二、课文　kèwén　Texts

A 05-01

yóukè: Qǐngwèn kěyǐ yòng nǎxiē fùkuǎn fāngshì zài jìngwài gòuwù xiāofèi ne?
游客：请问可以用哪些付款方式在境外购物消费呢？

dǎoyóu: Kěyǐ yòng wàihuì, lǚxíng zhīpiào huòzhě guójì xìnyòngkǎ.
导游：可以用外汇、旅行支票或者国际信用卡。

yóukè: Zhè sān zhǒng fāngshì yǒu shénme yōu-quēdiǎn ne?
游客：这三种方式有什么优缺点呢？

dǎoyóu: Wàihuì shǐyòng qilai fāngbiàn, shǒuxù jiǎndān, dànshì xiédài wàihuì chūjìng yǒu yí-
导游：外汇使用起来方便，手续简单，但是携带外汇出境有一

dìng de édù xiànzhì, ānquán yě shì gè wèntí. Lǚxíng zhīpiào bìzhǒng duō, miàn'é
定的额度限制，安全也是个问题。旅行支票币种多，面额

jiào gāo, shìhé xiédài shùliàng jiàodà de jīn'é, qí shǐyòng yě shì méiyǒu qīxiàn
较高，适合携带数量较大的金额，其使用也是没有期限

de. Dànshì gòumǎi lǚxíng zhīpiào yǐjí yòng bu wán de lǚxíng zhīpiào huíguó duìhuàn
的。但是购买旅行支票以及用不完的旅行支票回国兑换

shí, dōu xūyào kòuchú yí bùfen fèiyong, zài jìngwài xiāofèi shí, kěnéng yào shōu-
时，都需要扣除一部分费用，在境外消费时，可能要收

qǔ yídìng de shǒuxùfèi. Guójì xìnyòngkǎ tígōng de fúwù quánmiàn, xiédài ān-
取一定的手续费。国际信用卡提供的服务全面，携带安

quán, zài jìngwài xiāofèi kě zhíjiē shuākǎ, hái kěyǐ tòuzhī shǐyòng. Dànshì
全，在境外消费可直接刷卡，还可以透支使用。但是

guójì xìnyòngkǎ de shēnlǐng xūyào de shíjiān jiào cháng, shǒuxù jiào máfan, duì
国际信用卡的申领需要的时间较长，手续较麻烦，对

shēnlǐngzhě de shěnchá bǐjiào yángé. Lìngwài gēnjù xìnyòngkǎ de xìnyòng édù
申领者的审查比较严格。另外根据信用卡的信用额度

hé shēnqǐngzhě de xìnyòng qíngkuàng, hái yào jiǎonà yídìng bǎozhèngjīn, bìng shōuqǔ
和申请者的信用情况，还要缴纳一定保证金，并收取

yídìng de shǒuxùfèi.
一定的手续费。

译文 yìwén Text in English

Traveller: How can I pay for my purchases abroad?

Tour Guide: Foreign currency, traveler's checks or international credit cards are all OK.

Traveller: What are the advantages and disadvantages of these three methods?

Tour Guide: Foreign currency is easy to obtain and convenient to use, but there are limits on the amount you can carry abroad and carrying cash with you is also risky. Traveler's checks are available in a variety of currencies and in large denominations, and suitable for carrying larger amounts. There is no expiration date for their use. However, when purchasing traveler's checks and when exchanging the unused traveler's checks back home, a fee will be deducted, and a service fee may be charged for overseas consumption. Credit cards offer comprehensive services, are safe to carry, and can be used directly for overseas purchases, with the option for overdraft. However, applying for an international credit card can be time-consuming and complicated, and the applicants will be examined strictly. In addition, depending on the credit limit and credit standing of the applicant, a deposit is required and a service fee is charged.

普通词语 pǔtōng cíyǔ General Vocabulary 🎧 05-02

1.	付款	fù//kuǎn	v.	pay a sum of money
2.	消费	xiāofèi	v.	consume
3.	携带	xiédài	v.	carry
4.	限制	xiànzhì	v.	limit
5.	期限	qīxiàn	n.	deadline
6.	扣除	kòuchú	v.	deduct

专业词语 zhuānyè cíyǔ Specialized Vocabulary 🎧 05-03

1.	外汇	wàihuì	n.	foreign currency
2.	旅行支票	lǚxíng zhīpiào	phr.	traveler's check
3.	信用卡	xìnyòngkǎ	n.	credit card
4.	面额	miàn'é	n.	denomination
5.	兑换	duìhuàn	v.	exchange
6.	透支	tòuzhī	v.	overdraw
7.	申领	shēnlǐng	v.	apply
8.	审查	shěnchá	v.	examine
9.	信用额度	xìnyòng édù	phr.	credit limit
10.	缴纳	jiǎonà	v.	pay
11.	保证金	bǎozhèngjīn	n.	deposit
12.	手续费	shǒuxùfèi	n.	service charge

B 🎧 05-04

游客: 小爱，我刚去了一下儿卫生间，椅子上的电脑不见了。

导游: 那我们赶紧报警，调取这里的监控。

游客: 如果找不回来，可以找保险公司理赔吗？

导游: 可以的，你填写一下儿丢失物品的品名、金额等具体信息，我来出一份情况证明书，咱们旅行社盖章后，提交所有证明材料就可以向保险公司索赔了。

译文 yìwén Text in English

Traveller: Xiao Ai! I just went to the restroom for a moment, and the computer on the chair is missing.
Tour Guide: Let's call the police and check the surveillance footage here.
Traveller: If I can't get it back, can I ask the insurance company to settle the claim?
Tour Guide: Yes, you can. Please fill in some specific information about the lost item, such as the name, price, etc. I will issue a certificate of condition with our travel agency's stamp. After submitting all the supporting documents to the insurance company, you can file a claim.

普通词语 pǔtōng cíyǔ General Vocabulary 🎧 05-05

1.	卫生间	wèishēngjiān	n.	restroom
2.	外面	wàimiàn	n.	outside
3.	椅子	yǐzi	n.	chair
4.	赶紧	gǎnjǐn	adv.	quickly
5.	报警	bào//jǐng	v.	call the police
6.	监控	jiānkòng	v.	monitor
7.	丢失	diūshī	v.	lose

专业词语 zhuānyè cíyǔ Specialized Vocabulary 🎧 05-06

1.	保险	bǎoxiǎn	n.	insurance
2.	理赔	lǐpéi	v.	settle a claim
3.	证明书	zhèngmíngshū	n.	certificate
4.	旅行社	lǚxíngshè	n.	travel agency
5.	索赔	suǒpéi	v.	claim for compensation

三、视听说 shì-tīng-shuō Viewing, Listening, and Speaking

看视频，了解不属于保险理赔范围的物品和疾病，请在不属于理赔范围的物品和疾病下面打上×。
Watch the video to learn about the items and diseases not covered by insurance claim. Please mark an "×" below the items and diseases that are not covered.

bǎoxiǎn lǐpéi
保险理赔
Insurance Claims

导游专业知识 2
Tour Guide Expertise

yóupiào
① 邮票
Stamp

xiànjīn
② 现金
Cash

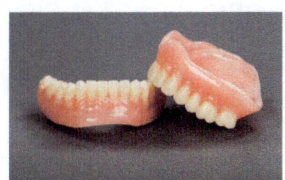

jiǎyá
③ 假牙
Artificial teeth

zhūbǎo
④ 珠宝
Jewelry

huáiyùn
⑤ 怀孕
Pregnancy

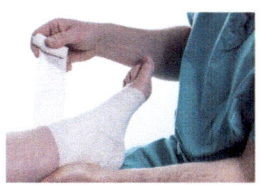

yìwài shòushāng
⑥ 意外 受伤
Accidental injury

shíwù zhōngdú
⑦ 食物 中毒
Food poisoning

hùzhào
⑧ 护照
Passport

说一说　Let's talk

说一说还有哪些不属于理赔范围的情况。　List other circumstances not covered by insurance claims.

四、学以致用　xuéyǐzhìyòng　Practicing What You Have Learnt

看视频，了解如何填写境外旅游保险单，选择正确的内容将下面的保险单填写完整。
Watch the video to learn how to fill out an overseas travel insurance policy, and then choose the correct answers to complete the following insurance policy.

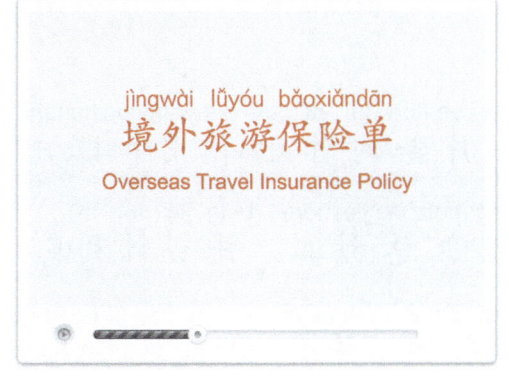

jìngwài lǚyóu bǎoxiǎndān
境外旅游保险单
Overseas Travel Insurance Policy

A. 柬埔寨 Jiǎnpǔzhài Cambodia
B. 总保险费 zǒng bǎoxiǎnfèi Total premium
C. 张三 Zhāng Sān Zhang San
D. 住院医疗 zhùyuàn yīliáo Hospitalization

① _____ ② _____ ③ _____ ④ _____

五、小知识 xiǎo zhīshi Tips

信用卡 Xìnyòngkǎ

账单日：发卡银行每月会对你的信用卡账户当期发生的各项交易、费用等进行汇总结算，并结计利息，计算你当期总欠款金额和最小还款额，并给你发送对账单。此日期即为你信用卡的账单日。

还款日：还款日一般是账单日后20天左右，不同银行略有不同，在19~25日之间。如果还款有困难，应最少还上最低还款额部分（一般为账单金额的5%或10%），否则将可能被全额罚息、收取滞纳金，并影响你的信用状况。

Credit Card

Billing day: The billing day is the day each month when the issuing bank settles all transactions and fees incurred during the current billing cycle in your credit card account. The bank calculates the interest, the total amount owed and the minimum amount of repayment, and sends you a statement of account. This is the billing day of your credit card.

Repayment date: The repayment date is generally about 20 days after the billing day, which may slightly vary depending on the bank, typically between the 19th and 25th day after the billing day. If you have trouble making a payment, you should at least pay the minimum amount of repayment (typically 5% or 10% of the bill amount), otherwise you may be subject to full interest charges, overdue fees and negative effects on your credit standing.

项目小结 *Item Summary*

词语 Vocabulary

普通词语　General Vocabulary

1.	付款	fù//kuǎn	v.	pay a sum of money
2.	消费	xiāofèi	v.	consume
3.	携带	xiédài	v.	carry
4.	限制	xiànzhì	v.	limit
5.	期限	qīxiàn	n.	deadline
6.	扣除	kòuchú	v.	deduct
7.	卫生间	wèishēngjiān	n.	restroom
8.	外面	wàimiàn	n.	outside
9.	椅子	yǐzi	n.	chair
10.	赶紧	gǎnjǐn	adv.	quickly

11.	报警	bào//jǐng	v.	call the police
12.	监控	jiānkòng	v.	monitor
13.	丢失	diūshī	v.	lose

专业词语　Specialized Vocabulary

1.	外汇	wàihuì	n.	foreign currency
2.	旅行支票	lǚxíng zhīpiào	phr.	traveler's check
3.	信用卡	xìnyòngkǎ	n.	credit card
4.	面额	miàn'é	n.	denomination
5.	兑换	duìhuàn	v.	exchange
6.	透支	tòuzhī	v.	overdraw
7.	申领	shēnlǐng	v.	apply
8.	审查	shěnchá	v.	examine
9.	信用额度	xìnyòng édù	phr.	credit limit
10.	缴纳	jiǎonà	v.	pay
11.	保证金	bǎozhèngjīn	n.	deposit
12.	手续费	shǒuxùfèi	n.	service charge
13.	保险	bǎoxiǎn	n.	insurance
14.	理赔	lǐpéi	v.	settle a claim
15.	证明书	zhèngmíngshū	n.	certificate
16.	旅行社	lǚxíngshè	n.	travel agency
17.	索赔	suǒpéi	v.	claim for compensation

jùzi 句子 Sentences

1. 可以用外汇、旅行支票或者国际信用卡在境外购物消费。
2. 境外旅行保险基本可分为人身安全和财产安全两种。
3. 当游客在境外旅游期间出现行李丢失、被盗，游客意外伤病和死亡时，可向保险公司索赔。

项目五　Item 5
国际时差知识　Knowledge on International Time Difference

题解　Introduction

1. 学习内容：时差概念及时差效应的影响。
   Learning content: The concept of jet lag and the influence of jet lag effect.
2. 知识目标：掌握与跟游客沟通、提供减少时差效应影响的预防措施有关的核心词语及表述。
   Knowledge objectives: To acquire the core words and expressions related to communicating with tourists and providing preventive measures to reduce the influences of jet lag effect.
3. 技能目标：能够看懂世界时区地图，会计算时区、时差和地方时。
   Skill objective: To be able to read the world time zone map and calculate time zone, time difference and local time.

一、热身　rèshēn　Warm-up

1. 请选择数字对应的名称。　Choose the names corresponding to the numbers.

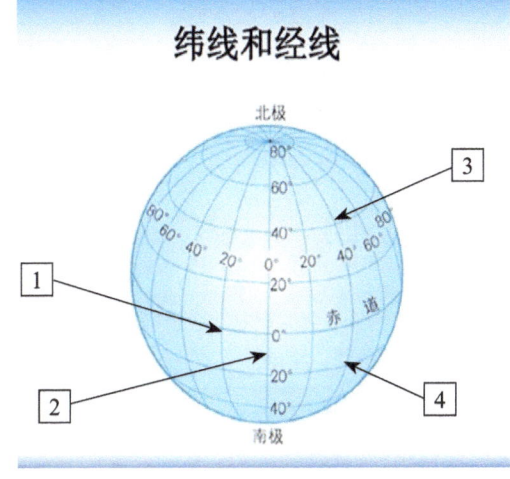

A. 经线 jīngxiàn　longitude

B. 纬线 wěixiàn　latitude

C. 赤道 chìdào　equator

D. 本初子午线 běnchū-zǐwǔxiàn　prime meridian

❶ _____　❷ _____

❸ _____　❹ _____

2. 看视频，了解时区的划分和计算方法，根据以下这些国家首都的经度判断它们所在的时区。
   Watch the video to learn about the division and calculation of time zones and determine the time zones of the following capitals according to their longitude.

shìjiè shíqū
世界时区
Time Zone

① Jīnbiān dōngjīng 104 dù   qū
  金边   东经 104 度   _____ 区
  Phnom Penh   104°E   time zone

② Běijīng dōngjīng 116 dù   qū
  北京   东经 116 度   _____ 区
  Beijing   116°E   time zone

③ Dōngjīng dōngjīng 139 dù   qū
  东京   东经 139 度   _____ 区
  Tokyo   139°E   time zone

④ Lúndūn dōngjīng 52 dù   qū
  伦敦   东经 52 度   _____ 区
  London   52°E   time zone

⑤ Niǔyuē xījīng 74 dù   qū
  纽约   西经 74 度   _____ 区
  New York   74°W   time zone

⑥ Mòsīkē dōngjīng 37 dù   qū
  莫斯科   东经 37 度   _____ 区
  Moscow   37°E   time zone

二、课文 kèwén Texts

A 🎧 06-01

dǎoyóu: Nǐmen hǎo! Huānyíng láidào Jiǎnpǔzhài shǒudū Jīnbiān.
导游：你们 好！欢迎 来到 柬埔寨 首都 金边。

yóukè: Nín hǎo! Qǐngwèn wǒmen jīntiān wǎnshang de ānpái shì shénme?
游客：您 好！请问 我们 今天 晚上 的 安排 是 什么？

导游：我们首先入住酒店。金边时间晚上六时我们在餐厅用餐，晚上八时我们将在酒店剧场观看一场精彩的柬埔寨文化演出。

游客：那金边时间是不是比北京时间晚了一个小时？

导游：是的，您说得很对。金边在东七区，北京在东八区，相差一个时区，所以金边时间比北京时间晚了一个小时。

游客：哦，我明白了，谢谢！

导游：国际时差可能会给大家带来一些不便，如果您有问题，请告诉我，我会全力帮您解决！

译文 yìwén Text in English

Tour Guide: Hello! Welcome to Phnom Penh, capital of Cambodia.

Tourist: Hello! May I know the arrangement of this evening?

Tour Guide: Sure. First, we'll check in the hotel, have our dinner at 6 p.m. Phnom Penh time, and then watch a wonderful Cambodian cultural performance in the hotel theater at 8 p.m.

Tourist: Is Phnom Penh time one hour later than Beijing Time?

Tour Guide: Yes, you are right. Phnom Penh is in GMT+7:00, while Beijing is in GMT+8:00, with one time zone apart. Therefore, Phnom Penh time is one hour later than Beijing Time.

Tourist: I see. Thank you.

Tour Guide: The international time difference may cause some inconvenience to you. If you have any problem, don't hesitate to tell me. I will try my best to help you.

普通词语 pǔtōng cíyǔ General Vocabulary 06-02

1.	首都	shǒudū	n.	capital
2.	安排	ānpái	n.	arrangement
3.	入住	rùzhù	v.	check in
4.	餐厅	cāntīng	n.	restaurant
5.	用餐	yòng//cān	v.	have a dinner
6.	剧场	jùchǎng	n.	theater
7.	精彩	jīngcǎi	adj.	wonderful
8.	演出	yǎnchū	n.	performance
9.	国际	guójì	adj.	international
10.	全力	quánlì	adv.	try one's best
11.	解决	jiějué	v.	solve

专业词语 zhuānyè cíyǔ Specialized Vocabulary 06-03

1.	柬埔寨	Jiǎnpǔzhài	pn.	Cambodia
2.	金边	Jīnbiān	pn.	Phnom Penh
3.	东七区	dōng qī qū	phr.	GMT+07:00
4.	相差	xiāng chà	phr.	differ
5.	时区	shíqū	n.	time zone
6.	时差	shíchā	n.	time difference

B 06-04

dǎoyóu: Nǐmen hǎo! Huānyíng chéngzuò fēijī cóng Zhōngguó láidào Jiǎnpǔzhài lǚyóu!
导游：你们好！欢迎乘坐飞机从中国来到柬埔寨旅游！

yóukè: Nín hǎo! Wǒ tīng biérén shuō yào dǎo shíchā, wǒmen xūyào ma?
游客：您好！我听别人说要倒时差，我们需要吗？

dǎoyóu: Nín yǒu shénme búshì de gǎnjué ma?
导游：您有什么不适的感觉吗？

游客: Wǒ hǎoxiàng méiyǒu shénme búshì de gǎnjué.
我好像没有什么不适的感觉。

导游: Shìde, yìbān lái shuō, yì liǎng ge xiǎoshí de shíchā, rén de shēnglǐ shang bìng bú huì chūxiàn míngxiǎn fǎnyìng, sān ge yǐshàng shíqū de fēixíng cái huì duì rénmen zàochéng yǐngxiǎng. Dāng shíchā dádào liù qī ge xiǎoshí de shíhou, shēnglǐ shang de fǎnyìng jiù bǐjiào míngxiǎn le.
是的,一般来说,一两个小时的时差,人的生理上并不会出现明显反应,三个以上时区的飞行才会对人们造成影响。当时差达到六七个小时的时候,生理上的反应就比较明显了。

游客: Yuánlái rúcǐ, xièxie nǐ de jiěshì!
原来如此,谢谢你的解释!

导游: Bú kèqì!
不客气!

译文 yìwén Text in English

Tour Guide: Hello! Welcome to Cambodia. You've arrived here from China for your trip.

Tourist: Hello! I wonder if we need to get over the jet lag.

Tour Guide: Are you feeling uncomfortable?

Tourist No, I am not.

Tour Guide: OK. Generally speaking, time difference of one or two hours does not have obvious influence on people physiologically. Usually the flight over three time zones can have an impact on people, and if the time difference is more than six or seven hours, people have obvious physiological reaction to it.

Tourist: Oh, I see. Thank you for your explanation.

Tour Guide: You are welcome.

普通词语 pǔtōng cíyǔ General Vocabulary 🎧 06-05

1.	乘坐	chéngzuò	v.	take or ride
2.	不适	búshì	adj.	uncomfortable
3.	生理	shēnglǐ	n.	physiology
4.	明显	míngxiǎn	adj.	obvious
5.	反应	fǎnyìng	n./v.	reaction; react
6.	影响	yǐngxiǎng	n.	influence
7.	解释	jiěshì	n.	explanation

专业词语 zhuānyè cíyǔ Specialized Vocabulary 🎧 06-06

1.	倒时差	dǎo shíchā	phr.	get over the jet lag

三、视听说 shì-tīng-shuō Viewing, Listening, and Speaking

看视频，了解倒时差的方法，请在可以减轻时差对人体造成影响的方法下面打上√，并试着说一说这些方法为什么能缓解。

Watch the video to learn the methods to get over the jet lag. Please tick the methods that can reduce the impact of jet lag on human body and explain why.

① tiáozhěng hǎo shuìmián móshì
  调整 好 睡眠 模式
  Adjusting the sleep mode

② jìn shí
  禁食
  Refrain from eating

③ chíxù liáotiānr
  持续 聊天儿
  Keeping chatting

④ tiáozhěng guāngzhào shíjiān
调整 光照 时间
Adjusting lighting time
_____

⑤ tīng yáogǔn yīnyuè
听 摇滚 音乐
Listening to rock and roll
_____

⑥ chī xīnlà shíwù
吃 辛辣 食物
Eating spicy food
_____

⑦ pèidài re-timer yǎnjìng
佩戴 re-timer 眼镜
Wearing re-timer glasses
_____

⑧ xuǎnzé héshì de hángbān
选择 合适 的 航班
Choosing the right flight
_____

说一说 Let's talk

说一说能减轻时差对人体影响的方法。
List the methods to reduce the impact of jet lag on human body.

四、学以致用 xuéyǐzhìyòng Practicing What You Have Learnt

看视频，了解时差和时间的计算方法，根据下面表格提供的信息，由柬埔寨首都金边的时间推算出不同国家首都的当地时间。

Watch the video to learn how to calculate time difference and local time, and calculate the local time of different capitals based on the information provided in the following table and Phnom Penh time.

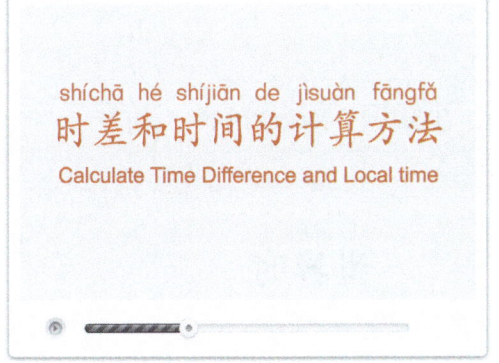

chéngshì 城市 City	Jīnbiān 金边 Phnom Penh	Běijīng 北京 Beijing	Dōngjīng 东京 Tokyo	Shǒu'ěr 首尔 Seoul	Huáshèngdùn 华盛顿 Washington	Lúndūn 伦敦 London	Xīní 悉尼 Sydney
shíqū 时区 Time zone	dōng qī qū 东 七 区 GMT+7	dōng bā qū 东 八 区 GMT +8	dōng jiǔ qū 东 九 区 GMT+9	dōng jiǔ qū 东 九 区 GMT+9	xī wǔ qū 西 五 区 GMT -5	língshíqū 零时区 GMT 0	dōng shí qū 东 十 区 GMT+10

Jīnbiān
金边
Phnom Penh

Xiànzài shì xiàwǔ 6 diǎn.
现在是下午6点。
It is 6 p.m. now.

Běijīng
❶ 北京＿＿＿＿
Beijing

Dōngjīng
❷ 东京＿＿＿＿
Tokyo

Shǒu'ěr
❸ 首尔＿＿＿＿
Seoul

Huáshèngdùn
❹ 华盛顿＿＿＿＿
Washington

Lúndūn
❺ 伦敦＿＿＿＿
London

Xīní
❻ 悉尼＿＿＿＿
Sydney

五、小知识　xiǎo zhīshi　**Tips**

Shìjièshí
世界时

"Shìjièshí" shì zhǐ "Gélínnízhì shíjiān". Gāi shíjiān shì yǐ Yīngguó Gélínnízhì
"世界时"是指"格林尼治时间"。该时间是以英国格林尼治

Tiānwéntái wéi biāozhǔn de, Gélínnízhì zài Lúndūn nán jiāo. Gāi dì shì dìlǐ jīngdù qǐdiǎn,
天文台为标准的，格林尼治在伦敦南郊。该地是地理经度起点，

xiànzài de zhè zhǒng xiǎoshí shíjiān dōu shì yǐ Gélínnízhì shíjiān wéi biāozhǔn de. Gè dì de
现在的这种小时时间都是以格林尼治时间为标准的。各地的

biāozhǔn shíjiān wéi Gélínnízhì shíjiān jiāshàng huò jiǎnqù shíqū zhōng suǒbiāo de xiǎoshí hé fēn-
标准时间为格林尼治时间加上或减去时区中所标的小时和分

zhōng shù shíchā.
钟数时差。

Universal Time

The "universal time" refers to the "Greenwich Mean Time", which is based on the Greenwich Observatory. Located in the southern suburb of London, Greenwich is the starting point of geographic longitudes. The current time is all based on the Greenwich Mean Time. The standard time of different places is the GMT plus (+) or minus (-) the time difference in hours and minutes indicated by the respective time zones.

项目小结 Item Summary

cíyǔ 词语 Vocabulary

普通词语 General Vocabulary

#				
1.	首都	shǒudū	n.	capital
2.	安排	ānpái	n.	arrangement
3.	入住	rùzhù	v.	check in
4.	餐厅	cāntīng	n.	restaurant
5.	用餐	yòngcān	v.	have a dinner
6.	剧场	jùchǎng	n.	theater
7.	精彩	jīngcǎi	n.	wonderful
8.	演出	yǎnchū	n.	performance
9.	国际	guójì	n.	international
10.	全力	quánlì	adj.	try one's best
11.	解决	jiějué	v.	solve
12.	乘坐	chéngzuò	v.	take or ride
13.	不适	búshì	adj.	uncomfortable
14.	生理	shēnglǐ	n.	physiology
15.	明显	míngxiǎn	adj.	obvious
16.	反应	fǎnyìng	n./v.	reaction; react
17.	影响	yǐngxiǎng	n.	influence
18.	解释	jiěshì	n.	explanation

专业词语 Specialized Vocabulary

#				
1.	柬埔寨	Jiǎnpǔzhài	pn.	Cambodia
2.	金边	Jīnbiān	pn.	Phnom Penh
3.	东七区	dōng qī qū	phr.	GMT+7:00
4.	相差	xiāng chà	phr.	differ

81

cíyǔ 词语 Vocabulary	5.	时区	shíqū	n.	time zone
	6.	时差	shíchā	n.	time difference
	7.	倒时差	dǎo shíchā	phr.	jet lag

jùzi
句子
Sentences

1. 金边在东七区，北京在东八区，相差一个时区。
2. 金边时间比北京时间晚了一个小时。
3. 原来如此，谢谢你的解释！

3

Wǒ wèilái de gōngzuò
我未来的工作
My Future Job

项目一　Item 1
景区接待服务　Reception Service at Scenic Spots

我的工作　My job

1. 规范与流程：学习景区接待服务流程、规范和服务用语。
   Procedures and Specifications: Learning the reception service procedures, specifications and service terms of a scenic spot.
2. 工作模块一：景区接待服务售票服务。
   Work Module 1: Reception service and ticketing service of a scenic spot.
3. 工作模块二：景区游览服务。
   Module 2: Scenic spot tour service.
4. 工作模块三：景区游客投诉服务。
   Module 3: Tourist complaint service at a scenic spot.

流程与规范　Procedures and Specifications

看视频，了解景区接待服务流程与规范，请判断下列服务属于哪个景区接待服务流程。
Watch the video to understand the reception service procedures and specifications in scenic spots, and determine which procedure the following reception service falls under.

A. Zhuānyè rényuán wèi kèrén jiǎngjiě běndì qìhòu、fēngtǔ rénqíng、zhùmíng tèchǎn jí jǐngqū jīběn qíngkuàng.
专业 人员 为 客人 讲解 本地 气候、风土 人情、著名 特产 及 景区 基本 情况。
Professionals explain the local climate, local customs, famous specialties and basic information of the scenic spot to guests.

B. Xiàng kèrén huò liánxìrén zhēngqiú yìjiàn, duì yìjiàn yào jíshí fǎnkuì.
向 客人 或 联系人 征求 意见，对 意见 要 及时 反馈。
Ask guests or contacts for opinions and give feedback in a timely manner.

C. Zài kèrén dàodá jǐngqū qián yì xiǎoshí nèi, ānpái tuǒdàng ménpiào、yòngcān、jǐngqū dǎoyóu děng jiēdài shìyí, zhǎngwò kèrén suǒ chéng chēliàng xìnxī jí dàodá shíjiān.
在 客人 到达 景区 前 一 小时 内，安排 妥当 门票、用餐、景区 导游 等 接待 事宜，掌握 客人 所 乘 车辆 信息 及 到达 时间。
Within one hour, before the guests arrive at the scenic spot, arrange the tickets, meals, tour guide at the scenic spot and other matters properly, and obtain the information about the guests' tour bus and arrival time.

我未来的工作 3
My Future Job

dàodá jǐngqū qián zhǔnbèi
❶ 到达景区前准备
Make preparations before the guests arrive at the scenic spot

dào jǐngqū ménkǒu yíngjiē kèrén
❷ 到景区门口迎接客人
Greet guests at the entrance of the scenic spot

zài jǐngqū nèi tígōng gè xiàng fúwù
❸ 在景区内提供各项服务
Provide services at the scenic spot

kèrén líkāi shíduàn fúwù
❹ 客人离开时段服务
Guest departure service

kèrén líkāi hòu de gōngzuò
❺ 客人离开后的工作
Work after the guests leave

jiéshù
❻ 结束
The end

A. _____

B. _____

C. _____

工作模块一 Working Module 1

景区接待服务售票服务。 Reception service and ticketing service of a scenic spot.

piàowù yùdìng
票务预订
Ticket Booking

piàowù yùdìng qúdào
票务 预订 渠道
Ticket booking channels

diànhuà dìngpiào
① **电话 订票**
Telephone booking

wǎng shang dìngpiào
② **网 上 订票**
Online booking

shòupiàochù dìngpiào
③ **售票处 订票**
Booking at the ticket office

lǚxíngshè dìngpiào
④ **旅行社 订票**
Travel agency booking

tuántǐ dìngpiào
⑤ **团体 订票**
Group booking

dìngpiào liúchéng
订票 流程
Booking process

tiánxiě yùdìng rìqī
① **填写 预订 日期**
Fill in the reservation date;

xuǎnzé yào dìnggòu de piàowù lèixíng hé shùliàng
② **选择 要 订购 的 票务 类型 和 数 量**
Select the type and quantity of tickets to book;

tiánxiě lǐngpiàorén xìnxī
③ **填写 领票人 信息**
Fill in the information of the ticket receiver;

quèrèn dìngdān
④ **确认 订单**
Confirm the order;

wǎng shang huò xiànchǎng zhīfù
⑤ **网 上 或 现场 支付**
Pay online or on site;

xiànchǎng qǔpiào
⑥ **现场 取票**
Pick up tickets on site.

我未来的工作
My Future Job

我的工作：

今天你将接待一个来自中国的旅游团，共有20人。他们将参观吴哥窟。现在请你确认下旅行团的情况，并填写这份确认单。

My job:

You will receive a group of 20 tourists from China today. They will visit Angkor Wat. Please confirm the information of the group and fill in this confirmation form.

quèrèndān

确认单

Confirmation Form

tuánhào

团号：

Group No.

dìqū huò guójí

地区或国籍：

Region or Nationality

cānguān rìqī 参观 日期 Date of visit	jǐngdiǎn míngchēng 景点 名称 Name of the scenic spot	rénshù（chéngrén/ értóng） 人数（成人/儿童） Number of people (adults/children)	yòngcān 用餐 Dining	bèizhù 备注 Notes
fèiyong héjì 费用 合计 Total cost				

旅行社（签章）： 　　　　　　　　景区:（签单）

Travel agency (seal): 　　　　　　Scenic spot (seal):

联系人： 　　　　　　　　　　　　联系人：

Contact: 　　　　　　　　　　　　Contact:

电话： 　　　　　　　　　　　　　电话：

Telephone: 　　　　　　　　　　　Telephone:

日期： 　　　　　　　　　　　　　日期：

Date: 　　　　　　　　　　　　　　Date:

工作模块二　Working Module 2

景区游览服务。Scenic service.

yóulǎn qián dǎoyóu fúwù
游览 前 导游服务
Pre-tour guide service

① gāi jǐngdiǎn de tíngliú shíjiān
该 景点 的 停留 时间
Length of stay in the scenic spot

② yóulǎn jiéshù hòu de jíhé dìdiǎn
游览 结束 后的 集合 地点
Gathering place after the tour

③ jǐngdiǎn de yóulǎn xiànlù
景点 的 游览 线路
Tour route in the scenic spot

④ jǐngdiǎn gàikuàng
景点 概 况
Overview of the scenic spot

yóulǎn guòchéng zhīzhōng
游览 过程 之中
During the tour

① dǎo yǔ yóu、jízhōng yǔ fēnsàn、láoyì xiāng jiéhé
导与游、集中与分散、劳逸 相 结合
Combine guiding and touring, group activities and individual exploration, as well as activity and rest;

② zuòhǎo tíxǐng gōngzuò, fángzhǐ yóukè zǒushī
做好提醒工作，防止 游客走失
Provide timely reminders to prevent tourists from getting lost.

导游工作用语：

Shǒuxiān hěn huānyíng dàjiā láidào Wúgē Kū, wǒ shì jīntiān dàilǐng dàjiā de dǎoyóu. Jīntiān
首先 很 欢迎大家来到吴哥窟，我是今天带领大家的导游。今天

wǒmen jiāng zài cǐ dì cānguān sān gè xiǎoshí, yóulǎn jiéshù hòu wǒmen zài yóukè zhōngxīn jíhé,
我们 将 在此地参观 三个小时，游览 结束后我们在 游客中心 集合，

qǐng dàjiā yídìng yào gēn tuán yìqǐ zǒu. Wǒmen jiāng huì yóulǎn Tǎpǔlóng Sì hé Nǚwáng Gōng,
请大家一定要跟 团 一起走。我们 将 会 游览 塔普隆寺和女王 宫，

yīnwèi shì lǚyóu wàngjì, zài jìnrù jǐngdiǎn shí kěnéng xūyào dàjiā páiduì, tiānqì yánrè,
因为是旅游旺季，在 进入 景点 时可能 需要大家排队，天气炎热，

qǐng dàjiā pèihé, bǎochí xīnqíng yúkuài, suǒyǒu de děngdài dōu shì wèile gèng hǎo de tǐyàn,
请大家 配合，保持心情 愉快，所有的 等待 都是为了 更 好的体验，

xīwàng jīnrì de lǚyóu néng dài gěi nǐmen měihǎo de tǐyàn.
希望 今日的旅游 能 带给你们美好的 体验。

3 我未来的工作
My Future Job

Useful expressions for tour guides:

First of all, welcome to Angkor Wat. I am your guide today. Today we are going to visit it for three hours. After the tour, we will gather at the Tourist Center. Please be sure to go with the group. We will visit Ta Prohm and Banteay Srei. As it is the peak tourist season now, we may need to queue up before entering the scenic spot. On such a hot day, please cooperate and keep a good mood. All the waiting is for a better experience. I hope this tour will be your unforgettable experience.

我的工作：

今天你接待了一个来自中国的旅游团，共有 20 人。他们将参观吴哥窟。现在请听一段有关吴哥窟的解说词，选择正确的答案填在横线上。

My job:

You will receive a group of 20 tourists from China today. They are going to visit Angkor Wat. Now listen to a commentary of Angkor Wat and choose the correct answers.

Wúgē Chéng
吴哥 城
Angkor Thom

Wúgē Chéng shì _____ de shǒudōu, shǐ jiàn yú _____ duō cì huǐ yú zhàn-
吴哥 城 是 _____ ❶ 的首都，始建于 _____ ❷ ，多次毁于战

huǒ, hòu jǐjīng chóngjiàn. Xiàncún de shì 12 shìjìmò, 13 shìjìchū yóu
火，后几经重建。现存的是12世纪末、13世纪初由 _____ ❸

suǒ jiàn.
所建。

89

中文+景点导游

吴哥城呈_____④_____，全城共有5道城门，4道通向城中心的_____⑤_____，还有一道通向皇宫的"胜利门"，城门上面是面向四方的_____⑥_____。5座城门外各有一座横跨_____⑦_____的大桥，桥的两旁置有_____⑧_____，每边27尊。神像高2.5米，呈_____⑨_____。

城内主要建筑物为巴戎寺，其核心部分是一组由16座相连_____⑩_____构成的建筑群，每座塔上满布_____⑪_____。除中央塔外，在两层台基的四周还排列着几十座形体相同的石塔，每座塔各有一座四面佛，他面带微笑，凝视远方，脸形酷似柬王摄耶拔摩七世的容貌。围绕着_____⑫_____上的建筑有两个同心的_____⑬_____，回廊上雕刻着大量_____⑭_____，主要以神话故事、当时重大的现实斗争和_____⑮_____为题材。

As the capital of the Angkor Dynasty, Angkor Thom was built in the 9th century and destroyed many times in wars. The existing one was built in the late 12th and early 13th centuries by King Jayavarman VII.

Angkor Thom is square with the five city gates, four of which lead to Bayon Temple in the center of the city, and one of which leads to the "Gate of Victory" of the palace, and above the gate is the Four-faced Buddha facing four directions. Outside each of five city gates is a bridge across the moat. On each side of the bridge are 27 stone Buddhas, each 2.5 meters high and seated on their heels.

The main building in the city is Bayon Temple, the core of which is an architectural complex consisting of 16 connected pagodas, each adorned with carvings. In addition to the central tower, there are dozens of stone towers of the same shape around the two-layered stylobate. Each tower has a Four-faced Buddha, who smiles and stares into the distance, and whose face resembles King Jayavarman VII. Two concentric square ambulatories surround the stylobate, on which a large number of reliefs are carved, mainly themed on fairy tales, major reality struggles of the time and daily life.

我未来的工作 3
My Future Job

Wúgē Wángcháo A. 吴哥 王朝	zhèngfāngxíng B. 正方形	Bāróng Sì C. 巴戎 寺
9 shìjì D. 9 世纪	Jiǎnwáng Shèyēbámó Qī Shì E. 柬王 摄耶拔摩七世	Sìmiànfó xiàng F. 四面佛 像
shídiāo shénxiàng G. 石雕 神像	hùchénghé H. 护城河	bǎotǎ I. 宝塔
guìzuòzhuàng J. 跪坐状	táijī K. 台基	diāokè L. 雕刻
rìcháng shēnghuó M. 日常 生活	fāngxíng huíláng N. 方形 回廊	fúdiāo O. 浮雕

① _____ ② _____ ③ _____ ④ _____

⑤ _____ ⑥ _____ ⑦ _____ ⑧ _____

⑨ _____ ⑩ _____ ⑪ _____ ⑫ _____

⑬ _____ ⑭ _____ ⑮ _____

工作模块三　Working Module 3

景区游客投诉服务。Tourist complaint service at a scenic spot.

```
                    liǎojiě yóukè tóusù de yuányīn
                    了解游客投诉的原因
                    Find out why tourists complain
                              │
                              ▼
                    shòulǐ tóusù de bùzhòu
                    受理投诉的步骤
                    Steps to handle complaints
```

qīngtīng 倾听 yóukè 游客 sùshuō 诉说 Listen to visitors	zhēnchéng 真诚 péilǐ 赔礼 dàoqiàn 道歉 Make sincere apologies	shōují 收集 zhěnglǐ xìnxī 整理信息 Collect and organize information	tíchū 提出 jiějué fāng'àn 解决方案 Propose solutions	xiéshāng 协商 jiějué fāng'àn 解决方案 Negotiate solutions	hòuxù 后续 gēnzōng fúwù 跟踪服务 Follow-up	shànhòu 善后 chǔlǐ shìyí 处理事宜 Remedial work

导游工作用语：

Xiàng nín zhèyàng dìwèi de rén ……
- 像您这样地位的人……

Rúguǒ nín kěyǐ …… wǒ huì hěn gǎnjī nín.
- 如果您可以……我会很感激您。

Yěxǔ nín kěyǐ zài …… fāngmiàn gěi wǒ yìxiē jiànyì.
- 也许您可以在……方面给我一些建议。

Nín zhēnde zài …… fāngmiàn bāngle wǒ yí gè máng.
- 您真的在……方面帮了我一个忙。

Qǐng nín …… yīnwèi nín zhēnde yǒu zhè fāngmiàn de zhuānyè zhīshi.
- 请您……因为您真的有这方面的专业知识。

Xiàng nín zhèyàng yǒu chéngjiù de rén ……
- 像您这样有成就的人……

Nín shuō de wánquán zhèngquè ……
- 您说得完全正确……

Wǒ wèi nín suǒ yùdào de wèntí ér gǎndào fēicháng bàoqiàn. Qǐng gàosu wǒ fāshēngle
我为您所遇到的问题而感到非常抱歉。请告诉我发生了

shénme shìqing ne?   Qǐng nín búyào zhāojí,   wǒ fēicháng lǐjiě   nín de xīnqíng,   wǒmen yídìng huì
什么 事情 呢？请 您 不要 着急，我 非常 理解 您 的 心情，我们 一定 会
   jiéjìn   quánlì   wéi nín   jiějué de.   Wǒmen huì jiāng nín shuō de qíngkuàng jǐnkuài fǎnyìng gěi xiāng-
竭尽 全力 为 您 解决 的。我们 会 将 您 说 的 情况 尽快 反映 给 相
guān bùmén qù zuò gǎijìn,   xièxie nín de lǐjiě hé zhīchí,   wǒmen jiāng búduàn gǎijìn fúwù,
关 部门 去 做 改进，谢谢 您 的 理解 和 支持，我们 将 不断 改进 服务，
ràng nín mǎnyì.
让 您 满意。

Useful expressions for tour guides:

- A man in your position...
- If you could... I would be very grateful to you.
- Perhaps you can give me some advice on…
- You really did me a favor.
- Would you please... because you are a specialist in this field?
- The high achievers like you...
- You're absolutely right...

    I am very sorry for the problems you have encountered. Please tell me what happened. Please don't worry. I fully understand your feelings and we will try our best to solve it for you. We will report what you've said to relevant departments for improvement as soon as possible. Thank you for your understanding and support. We will continue to improve our service to your satisfaction.

我的工作：

今天你将接待一个来自中国的旅游团，共有20人。他们将参观吴哥窟。游览结束后，请让旅客填写满意度调查表，并及时解决调查表上的问题和建议。

My job:

You are going to receive a group of 20 tourists from China today. They will visit Angkor Wat. After the tour, please ask them to fill in the satisfaction questionnaire, and respond to the problems and suggestions in time.

对导游的投诉处理和满意度调查 Tour Guide Complaint Handling and Satisfaction Survey

尊敬的游客：

　　非常感谢您在珍贵的旅游过程中填写这份意见调查表。您的宝贵意见将作为评估本景区游客满意度的重要参考依据。

　　谢谢您的配合与支持，祝您旅游愉快！

Dear visitors,

　　Thank you very much for filling in this questionnaire during your trip. Your valuable opinions will be taken as an important reference to evaluate the tourist satisfaction of this scenic spot.

　　Thank you for your cooperation and support. Wish you a pleasant trip.

diàochá xiàngmù 调查 项目 Survey item	hěn mǎnyì 很 满意 Quite satisfied	mǎnyì 满意 Satisfied	yìbān 一般 So-so	bù mǎnyì 不 满意 Not satisfied
wàibù jiāotōng zhǐyǐn 外部 交通 指引 External traffic guidance				
nèibù yóulǎn xiànlù 内部 游览 线路 Internal tour itinerary arrangement				
guānjǐng shèshī 观景 设施 Facilities for sightseeing				
lùbiāo zhǐshì 路标 指示 Signs for directions				
jǐngwù jièshàopái 景物 介绍牌 Introduction boards				
xuānchuán zīliào 宣传 资料 Publicity materials				
dǎoyóu jiǎngjiě 导游 讲解 Tour guide service				
fúwù zhìliàng 服务 质量 Quality of service				
huánjìng wèishēng 环境 卫生 Environmental health				

（续表）

diàochá xiàngmù 调查 项目 Survey item	hěn mǎnyì 很 满意 Quite satisfied	mǎnyì 满意 Satisfied	yìbān 一般 So-so	bù mǎnyì 不 满意 Not satisfied
yóukè fúwù zhōngxīn 游客 服务 中心 Tourist Service Center				
jǐngqū cèsuǒ 景区 厕所 Toilets				
shāngpǐn gòuwù 商品 购物 Shopping				
cānyǐn huò shípǐn 餐饮 或 食品 Food & beverage				
lǚyóu zhìxù 旅游 秩序 Public order				
jǐngqū bǎohù 景区 保护 Scenic spot protection				
zǒngtǐ yìnxiàng 总体 印象 Overall impression				
qítā yìjiàn hé jiànyì 其他意见和建议： Other comments and suggestions				

项目二 Item 2
景区解说服务 Commentary Service at Scenic Spots

我的工作 My job

1. 规范与流程：学习景区解说服务流程、规范和服务用语。
   Procedures and Specifications: Learning the interpretation service procedures, specifications and service terms of scenic spots.
2. 工作模块一：旅游景区环境解说服务。
   Work Module 1: Environmental interpretation service of tourist attractions.
3. 工作模块二：旅游吸引物解说服务。
   Module 2: Interpretation services for tourist attractions.
4. 工作模块三：旅游管理解说服务。
   Module 3: Tourism management interpretation service.

流程与规范 Procedures and Specifications

看视频，了解景区解说服务流程与规范，请判断下列解说服务属于景区哪个解说服务流程。
Watch the video to understand scenic spot interpretation service procedures and specifications, and determine which procedure the following interpretation service falls under.

liúchéng yǔ guīfàn
流程与规范
Procedures and Specifications

我未来的工作
My Future Job 3

A. Yào xiān huòdé xǔkě cái kěyǐ pāi Jiǎnpǔzhàirén huò sēnglǚ de zhàopiàn.
要先获得许可才可以拍柬埔寨人或僧侣的照片。
You need to obtain permission before taking photos of Cambodians or monks.

B. Jiǎnpǔzhài lǚyóu jǐngdiǎn zhòngduō, rú Wúgē Kū, Jīnbiān Wánggōng, Dúlì Jìniànbēi, Zhōngxíng Tǎ,
柬埔寨旅游景点众多，如吴哥窟、金边王宫、独立纪念碑、钟形塔、
Bīnjiāng Gōngyuán děng.
滨江公园等。
There are many tourist attractions in Cambodia, such as Angkor Wat, the Royal Palace in Phnom Penh, the Independence Monument, Wat Phnom, the Riverside Park, etc.

C. Jiǎnpǔzhài wèiyú Zhōngnán Bàndǎo, xībù jí xīběibù yǔ Tàiguó jiērǎng, dōngběibù yǔ Lǎowō jiāojiè,
柬埔寨位于中南半岛，西部及西北部与泰国接壤，东北部与老挝交界，
dōngbù jí dōngnánbù yǔ Yuènán pílín, nánbù zé miànxiàng Tàiguó Wān.
东部及东南部与越南毗邻，南部则面向泰国湾。
Cambodia is located in Indochina Peninsula, bordering Thailand in the west and northwest, Laos in the northeast, Vietnam in the east and southeast, and facing the Gulf of Thailand in the south.

中文 + 景点导游

① 准备阶段：自身准备、知识准备、计划准备
zhǔnbèi jiēduàn: zìshēn zhǔnbèi、zhīshi zhǔnbèi、jìhuà zhǔnbèi
Preparation stage: making self-preparation, knowledge preparation and plan preparation.

② 迎接服务阶段：致欢迎辞、景区环境解说
yíngjiē fúwù jiēduàn: zhì huānyíngcí、jǐngqū huánjìng jiěshuō
Welcoming stage: making a welcoming speech and a scenic spot environment interpretation

A. _____

③ 游览阶段：景点解说
yóulǎn jiēduàn: jǐngdiǎn jiěshuō
Visiting stage: making scenic spot interpretation

B. _____

C. _____

④ 景区管理解说
jǐngqū guǎnlǐ jiěshuō
Making a scenic spot management interpretation

⑤ 结束
jiéshù
The end

工作模块一　　Working Module 1

旅游景区环境解说服务。**Environmental interpretation service at scenic spots.**

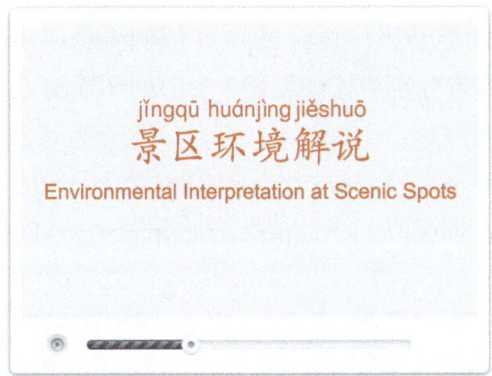

Lǚyóu jǐngqū huánjìng jiěshuō nèiróng:
旅游 景区 环境 解说 内容：
Content of scenic spot environmental interpretation:

　　zìrán huánjìng jiěshuō
❶ 自然 环境 解说
　　Natural environmental interpretation

　　shèhuì huánjìng jiěshuō
❷ 社会 环境 解说
　　Social environmental interpretation

　　wénhuà huánjìng jiěshuō
❸ 文化 环境 解说
　　Cultural environmental interpretation

　　jīngjì huánjìng jiěshuō
❹ 经济 环境 解说
　　Economic environmental interpretation

Lǚyóu jǐngqū huánjìng jiěshuō zhòngdiǎn:
旅游 景区 环境 解说 重点：
Focus of scenic spot environmental interpretation:

　　Yǐ zìrán huánjìng jiěshuō wéi zhòngdiǎn de jǐngqū:　zìrán bǎohùqū、zhíwùyuán、fēngjǐng míngshèng qū děng;
❶ 以自然 环境 解说 为 重点 的 景区：自然保护区、植物园、风景 名胜 区等；
　　Scenic spots with focus on natural environmental interpretation: natural reserves, botanical gardens, scenic areas, etc.;

② 以文化环境解说为重点的景区：博院馆、寺庙观堂、文化艺术类景区等；

Scenic spots with focus on cultural environmental interpretation: museums, temples, cultural and art attractions, etc.;

③ 以社会、经济环境解说为重点的景区：主题公园、游乐场，以及工业、农业、经贸、科教、军事、体育类景区。

Scenic spots with focus on social and economic environmental interpretation: theme parks, amusement parks, and industrial, agricultural, economic and trade, scientific and educational, military and sports attractions.

> **我的工作：**
> 今天你将接待一个来自中国的旅游团，共有20人。他们将参观柬埔寨以下景点。现在请你根据各个景点情况，判断以下景点分别应该侧重哪个方面的环境解说。
>
> **My job:**
> You will receive a group of 20 tourists from China today. They will visit the following scenic spots in Cambodia. Please determine which environmental interpretation should be focused on for the following scenic spots.

旅游景区环境解说重点

Focus of scenic spot environmental interpretation

景区	自然环境 Natural environment	社会环境 Social environment	文化环境 Cultural environment	经济环境 Economic environment
吴哥窟 Angkor Wat				
洞里萨湖 Tonle Sap				
柬埔寨国家博物馆 National Museum of Cambodia				

（续表）

景区 jǐngqū	自然环境 zìrán huánjìng Natural environment	社会环境 shèhuì huánjìng Social environment	文化环境 wénhuà huánjìng Cultural environment	经济环境 jīngjì huánjìng Economic environment
桔井 Jújǐng Kratie				
西哈努克海滩 Xīhānǔkè Hǎitān Sihanoukville Beach				

工作模块二 Working Module 2

旅游吸引物解说服务。Interpretation services for tourist attractions.

旅游吸引物 Lǚyóu xīyǐnwù
Tourist attractions

旅游吸引物指自然界和人类社会中，能对游客产生吸引力的各种事物和因素。

Tourist attractions refer to all kinds of things and factors that attract tourists in nature and human society.

旅游吸引物解说：

Interpretation of tourist attractions:

旅游吸引物解说是对旅游景区内各景点的解说，主要向游客展示景区的各类旅游景观以及已开发的景点景物，包括自然旅游景观、社会文化景观和节日活动景观等。

Tourist attraction interpretation is the interpretation of each scenic spot in the scenic area, mainly to show tourists all kinds of landscapes and scenic spots that have been developed, including natural landscapes, social and cultural landscapes and festival activity landscapes.

导游工作用语：

欢迎大家来到柬埔寨，我是今天带领大家的导游。下面我给大家简单介绍下柬埔寨吸引游客们的地方。柬埔寨的文化景观

shífēn fēngfù, běibù de Xiānlì Shì jìnjiāo yǒu jǔshì wénmíng de shìjiè yíchǎn Wúgē Kū, zài
十分丰富，北部的暹粒市近郊有举世闻名的世界遗产吴哥窟，在

zhōngbù de Jīnbiān yǒu dàliàng de fójiào sìmiào. Xībù yǒu Dōngnányà zuì dà de dànshuǐhú
中部的金边有大量的佛教寺庙。西部有东南亚最大的淡水湖

Dònglǐsà Hú, nánbù de Xīhānǔkè Shì kě xiǎngshòu yángguāng yǔ měilì de hǎitān. Chúle
洞里萨湖，南部的西哈努克市可享受阳光与美丽的海滩。除了

zhèxiē rénwén hé zìrán jǐngguān zhīwài, rúguǒ lái de zhèngshì shíhòu, hái néng gǎnshòu xià
这些人文和自然景观之外，如果来的正是时候，还能感受下

Jiǎnpǔzhài de hěnduō jiérì huódòng, rú Jiǎnpǔzhài Xīnnián, Fódàn Jié, Yùgēng Jié, Sòngshuǐ
柬埔寨的很多节日活动，如柬埔寨新年、佛诞节、御耕节、送水

Jié děng.
节等。

Useful expressions for tour guides:
　　Welcome to Cambodia. I am your tour guide today. Now I will give you a brief introduction to the tourist attractions in Cambodia. Cambodia is abundant in cultural landscapes, such as the world cultural heritage Angkor Wat in the suburb of Siem Reap in the north of Cambodia, and numerous Buddhist temples in Phnom Penh in the center of Cambodia. Tonle Sap in the west is the largest freshwater lake in Southeast Asia, while Sihanoukville in the south offers sunshine and beautiful beaches. In addition to these cultural and natural landscapes, you can also experience many festival activities in Cambodia if you come here at the right time, such as the Khmer New Year, Visakha Puja, Chat Preah Nengkal, Bon Om Tuk, etc.

我的工作：
　　今天你将接待一个来自中国的旅游团，共有20人。他们将参观金边王宫。现在请听一段有关金边王宫的解说词，选择正确的答案填在横线上。

My job:
　　You will receive a group of 20 tourists from China today. They are going to visit the Royal Palace of Phnom Penh. Now listen to a commentary of the Royal Palace of Phnom Penh, and choose the correct answers to fill in the blanks.

Jīnbiān Wánggōng
金边 王宫
The Royal Palace of Phnom Penh

我未来的工作 3
My Future Job

金边王宫也称四臂湾大王宫，因位于_____①、洞里萨河与巴萨河的交汇处而得名，是诺罗敦国王于_____②年建造的，充满高棉传统建筑风格和_____③。

金边王宫是柬埔寨国王的_____④，由一组金色屋顶、黄墙环绕的建筑组成，造型精美，_____⑤。包括查雅殿、金殿、银殿、舞乐殿、宝物殿等_____⑥多座大小宫殿，宫殿均有尖塔，代表_____⑦；殿身以黄、白两色为主，黄色代表_____⑧，白色代表_____⑨。建筑回廊上是仿吴哥寺的华丽浮雕_____⑩，描绘了历代王朝功绩和宗教故事。

The Royal Palace of Phnom Penh, also known as the Grand Palace of the Four Arms Bay, got its name because of its location at the confluence of Mekong River, Tonle Sap River and Bassac River. Built by King Norodom from 1866 to 1870, it is characterized by traditional Khmer architectural style and religious features.

As the palace of the King of Cambodia, the Royal Palace consists of a group of buildings with golden roofs surrounded by yellow walls, and it is resplendent and magnificent in exquisite shape. It has more than 20 big and small palaces, including Chaya Pagoda, Golden Pagoda, Silver Pagoda, Wele Pagoda and Treasure Pagoda. The pagodas all have spires, representing prosperity; the pagoda bodies are mainly in yellow and white, with yellow representing Buddhism and white Brahmanism. On the ambulatories are gorgeous relief frescoes replicating Angkor Wat, depicting the achievements of past dynasties and religious stories.

gōngdiàn	Méigōng Hé	fánróng	Póluóménjiào
A. 宫殿	B. 湄公河	C. 繁荣	D. 婆罗门教

	bìhuà		zōngjiào sècǎi
E. 1866—1870	F. 壁画	G. 20	H. 宗教色彩

Fójiào	jīnbìhuī-huáng
I. 佛教	J. 金碧辉煌

❶ _____   ❷ _____   ❸ _____   ❹ _____

❺ _____   ❻ _____   ❼ _____   ❽ _____

❾ _____   ❿ _____

工作模块三　Working Module 3

旅游管理解说服务。Tourism management interpretation service.

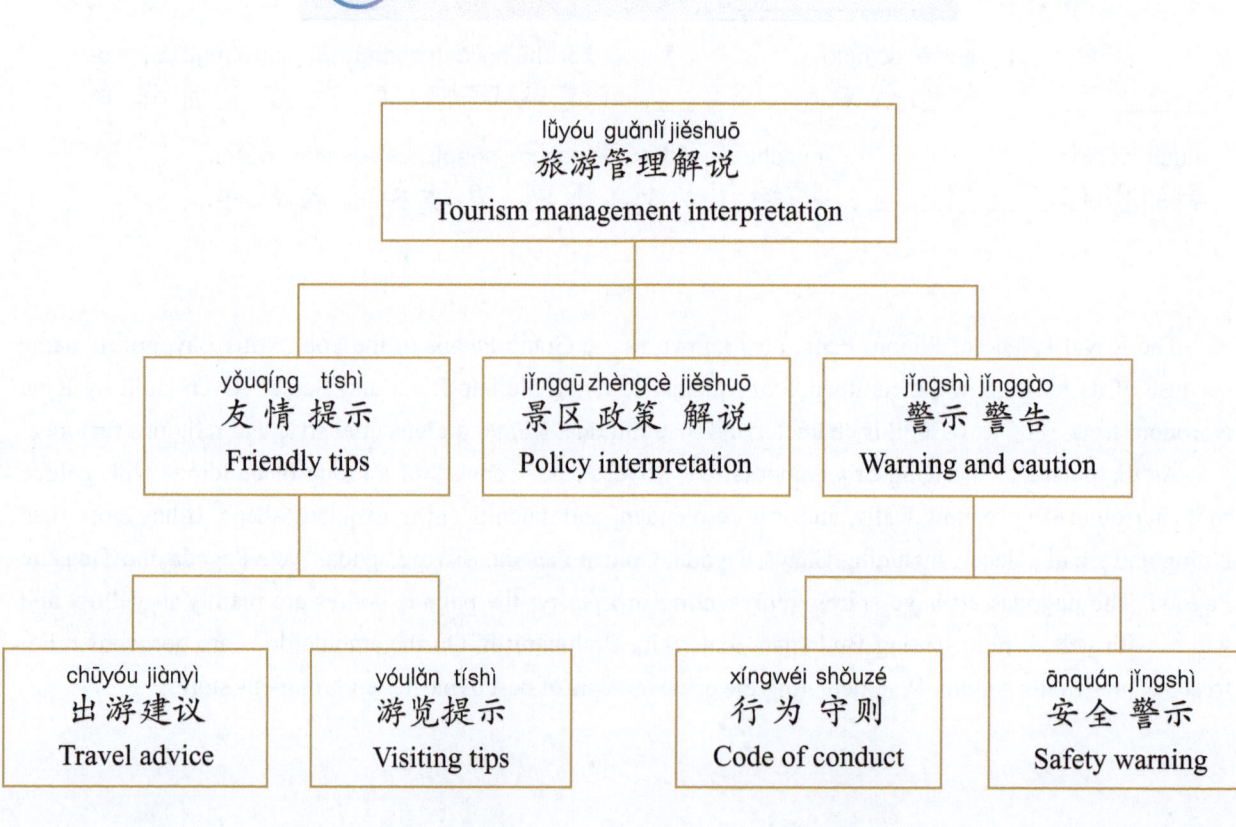

旅游管理解说 lǚyóu guǎnlǐ jiěshuō
Tourism management interpretation

- 友情提示 yǒuqíng tíshì — Friendly tips
- 景区政策解说 jǐngqū zhèngcè jiěshuō — Policy interpretation
- 警示警告 jǐngshì jǐnggào — Warning and caution

- 出游建议 chūyóu jiànyì — Travel advice
- 游览提示 yóulǎn tíshì — Visiting tips
- 行为守则 xíngwéi shǒuzé — Code of conduct
- 安全警示 ānquán jǐngshì — Safety warning

导游工作用语：

- 柬埔寨超市、大餐厅、酒店等地方用美金较多，市场上的人、摊贩都用柬币，建议随身携带适量柬币。

- 进佛寺参观时，要衣着得体整洁，需着长衣裤，免冠脱鞋。

- 柬埔寨是一个小费制度国家，当地司机和酒店服务人员帮忙提行李或到客房送水、献花等，出于礼貌是要给小费的。

- 柬埔寨政府对环境保护很重视，公共场所不准吸烟，否则会被罚款。

- 柬埔寨禁赌，即使在酒店房间内也请勿进行赌博类活动。

- 夜间或自由活动时间若需自行外出，请告知领队，并应特别注意安全。

Useful expressions for tour guides:

US dollars are used in most Cambodian supermarkets, large restaurants and hotels, etc. while the Cambodian currency is used in markets and by vendors, etc. You are advised to carry an appropriate amount of Cambodian currency with you.

When visiting a Buddhist temple, you should dress appropriately and neatly, wear long trousers, and take off your hat and shoes.

Cambodia is a country adopting tipping system. The local driver and hotel staff who assist with luggage, deliver water to your room, or present flowers, etc., should be given a tip as a courtesy.

The Cambodian government attaches great importance to environmental protection. Smoking is not allowed in public places, otherwise you will be fined.

Gambling is prohibited in Cambodia. Do not engage in gambling activities, even in hotel rooms.

If you need to go out by yourself at night or during free time, please inform the team leader and pay special attention to safety.

中文＋景点导游

我的工作：

今天你将接待一个来自中国的旅游团，共有20人。他们将参观柬埔寨的一些著名景点。请判断下列旅游管理解说是否恰当，在恰当的旅游管理解说用语处打√。

My job:

You are going to receive a group of 20 tourists from China today. They will visit some famous scenic spots in Cambodia. Please determine whether the following tourism management interpretations are appropriate or not, and tick the appropriate ones.

旅游管理解说用语　Tourism management interpretation

❶ Páizi shang xiě de ānquán tíshì, nǐmen zìjǐ kàn.
牌子上写的安全提示，你们自己看。_____
Please read the safety tips on the sign.

❷ Yóukè bìxū zūnjìng sēnglǚ.
游客必须尊敬僧侣。_____
Visitors must show respect to monks.

❸ Dàjiā kěyǐ yòng shǒu chùmō fóxiàng gǎnshòu yíxiàr.
大家可以用手触摸佛像感受一下儿。_____
You can touch the Buddha with your hand and feel it.

❹ Tōuqiè wénwù huò pòhuài gǔjì, dōu shì fànzuì de xíngwéi, jiāng shòudào fǎlǜ zhìcái.
偷窃文物或破坏古迹，都是犯罪的行为，将受到法律制裁。_____
Stealing cultural relics or destroying historical sites is a crime and will be punished by law.

❺ Jiǎnpǔzhài dāngdìrén rènwéi zuǒshǒu shì bù jié de xiàngzhēng, yòng zuǒshǒu ná dōngxi huò shíwù, dōu shì bù dǒng
柬埔寨当地人认为左手是不洁的象征，用左手拿东西或食物，都是不懂
lǐmào de biǎoxiàn. Yīncǐ, qǐng wù shǐyòng zuǒshǒu chùmō huò chuándì wùpǐn gěi dāngdìrén.
礼貌的表现。因此，请勿使用左手触摸或传递物品给当地人。_____
Local Cambodians believe that the left hand is a symbol of uncleanness, and it is impolite to use the left hand to hold things or food. Therefore, do not touch or pass things to locals with your left hand.

项目三　Item 3
景区商业服务　Commercial Services at Scenic Spot

我的工作　My job

1. 规范与流程：学习景区商业服务流程、规范和服务用语。
   Procedures and Specifications: Learning the commercial service procedures, specifications and service terms of scenic spots.
2. 工作模块一：景区商业服务购物服务。
   Module 1: Scenic spot shopping service.
3. 工作模块二：景区商业服务餐饮服务。
   Module 2: Scenic spot catering service.
4. 工作模块三：景区商业服务住宿服务。
   Module 3: Scenic spot accommodation service.

流程与规范　Procedures and Specifications

听录音，了解景区餐饮服务流程与规范，判断下列服务属于哪个景区餐饮服务流程。
Listen to the recording to learn about the scenic spot catering service procedures and specifications, and determine which procedure the following catering service falls under.

liúchéng yǔ guīfàn
流 程 与 规 范
Procedures and Specifications

我未来的工作
My Future Job　3

中文＋景点导游

A. Yào ànzhào bīnkè yāoqiú, tígōng càidiǎn dǎbāo fúwù, bìng jiāng bīnkè sòng zhì cāntīng ménkǒu.
要按照宾客要求，提供菜点打包服务，并将宾客送至餐厅门口。
You should pack the leftovers as required by the guests, and send them off to the gate of the restaurant.

B. Yīng zhǔdòng xiàng qián yíngjiē bīnkè, wèi bīnkè lā yǐ ràngzuò, sòngshang cāntīng càidān hé jiǔshuǐdān.
应主动向前迎接宾客，为宾客拉椅让座，送上餐厅菜单和酒水单。
You should take the initiative to greet the guests, pull out chairs, and offer them the menu and drinks list.

C. Yīng rèqíng zhǔdòng de xiàng bīnkè jièshào càipǐn tèdiǎn, shì qíngkuàng tíxǐng bīnkè shìliàng yòngcān.
应热情主动地向宾客介绍菜品特点，视情况提醒宾客适量用餐。
You should introduce the characteristics of the dishes to the guests enthusiastically and actively, and remind the guest to dine moderately as the case may be.

D. Yào jíshí wèi bīnkè zhēn dào jiǔshuǐ, huàn gǔdié děng.
要及时为宾客斟倒酒水、换骨碟等。
You should pour drinks and replace bone plates for the guests in a timely manner.

dàodá cāntīng qián de zhǔnbèi
❶ 到达餐厅前的准备
Make preparations before the guests arrive at the restaurant

A. _____

dào cāntīng ménkǒu yíngjiē kèrén
❷ 到餐厅门口迎接客人
Greet guests at the gate of the restaurant

B. _____

C. _____

zài cāntīng nèi diǎndān fúwù
❸ 在餐厅内点单服务
Guest ordering service

D. _____

108

```
┌─────────────────────────────┐
│  zài cāntīng nèi yòngcān fúwù │
│ ❹ 在餐厅内用餐服务           │
│   Guest dining service       │
└─────────────────────────────┘
```

```
┌─────────────────────────────┐
│  kèrén líkāi shí de fúwù     │
│ ⑮ 客人离开时的服务           │
│   Guest departure service    │
└─────────────────────────────┘
```

工作模块一　　Working Module 1

景区商业服务购物服务。Scenic spot shopping service.

jǐng qū gòuwù jiē dài fú wù zōngzhǐ:　　gùkè zhìshàng　fúwù　dì-yī
景区购物接待服务宗旨：顾客至上、服务第一
Tenets of shopping service in scenic spots: Customer first, service first

jǐngqū gòuwù jiēdài fúwù liúchéng:
景区购物接待服务流程：
Procedures of shopping service in scenic spots:

huānyíng kèrén
① 欢迎客人
Welcome the guests

zhǎnshì fúwù
② 展示服务
Display service

yànxiāo shāngpǐn
③ 验销商品
Inspect and sell the goods

bāozhuāng chéngjiāo
④ 包装 成交
Package the goods

sòngbié kèrén
⑤ 送别客人
See the guests off

我的工作：

今天你将接待一个来自中国的旅游团，共有20人。他们将在马德望中央市场进店购物，其中有很多女性对柬埔寨的丝绸很感兴趣。现在请你根据购物接待服务流程，将下面对话进行排序。

My job:

You will receive a group of 20 tourists from China today. They will shop in Battambang Psar Nat Market. Many women are very interested in Cambodian silk. Please sequence the following conversations according to the shopping service procedures.

A. Nǐ hǎo, tīngshuō Jiǎnpǔzhài de gōngyìpǐn zuògōng jīngzhàn, hěn yǒu míngqì, wǒmen xiǎng dài xiē huí qù. Nǐ néng wèi wǒmen tuījiàn diǎnr shénme ma?
你好，听说柬埔寨的工艺品做工精湛，很有名气，我们想带些回去。你能为我们推荐点儿什么吗？
Hello! We've heard that Cambodian handicrafts are exquisite and famous. We want to take some home. Can you recommend some for us?

B. Jìrán rúcǐ, wǒmen xiǎng kànkan sīchóu. Zhè tiáo lǜsè de duōshao qián?
既然如此，我们想看看丝绸。这条绿色的多少钱？
Well, let's take a look at silk. How much is this green one?

C. Nín hǎo, huānyíng guānglín. Yǒu shénme kěyǐ wèi nín xiàoláo de, fūrén?
您好，欢迎光临。有什么可以为您效劳的，夫人？
Hello! Welcome to our shop. What can I do for you, madam?

D. Hǎo de, shì 5 měijīn.
好的，是5美金。
OK. Here's five dollars.

110

3 我未来的工作
My Future Job

E. **Wǒmen shāngdiàn yǒu fēicháng duō de gōngyìpǐn, lìrú mùdiāo、sīchóu、yínqì、pídiāo děng děng. Nín kǎolǜ hǎo mǎi diǎnr shénme le ma?**
我们商店有非常多的工艺品，例如木雕、丝绸、银器、皮雕等等。您考虑好买点儿什么了吗？
There are a lot of handicrafts in our shop, such as wood carving, silk, silverware, leather carving and so on. Have you decided what to buy?

F. **Hái méiyǒu. Búguò wǒ xiǎng yīnggāi shì jí jù Jiǎnpǔzhài tèsè de, érqiě yào biànyú xiédài.**
还没有。不过我想应该是极具柬埔寨特色的，而且要便于携带。
Not yet. But I think it should be with Cambodian characteristics and easy to carry.

G. **Nà wǒ jiànyì nín kěyǐ mǎi xiē sīchóu huòzhě xiǎoxíng de mùdiāo, bùjǐn měiguān、shíyòng, yě biànyú xiédài.**
那我建议您可以买些丝绸或者小型的木雕，不仅美观、实用，也便于携带。
I suggest you buy some silk or small wood carvings, which are not only beautiful, practical, but also easy to carry.

H. **Xièxie, zhè shì nín de zhǎolíng, qǐng shāo děng, wǒ bāng nín bǎ tā bāo qilai. Xièxie nín de guānggù.**
谢谢，这是您的找零，请稍等，我帮您把它包起来。谢谢您的光顾。
Thank you. Here's your change. Just a moment, please. I'll wrap it for you. Thank you for your patronage.

I. **3 měijīn.**
3 美金。
Three dollars.

工作模块二 Working Module 2

景区商业服务餐饮服务。**Scenic spot catering service.**

jǐngqū cānyǐn fúwù de jīběn yāoqiú:
景区餐饮服务的基本要求：
Basic requirements for catering services in scenic spots:

① wèishēng jiéjìng
  卫生洁净
  Cleanliness and hygiene

② fúwù xùnsù
  服务迅速
  Fast service

③ jiàgé gōngdào
  价格公道
  Reasonable price

④ zūnzhòng yóukè
  尊重游客
  Respect for tourists

⑤ yíngzào fēnwéi
  营造氛围
  Creating a pleasant atmosphere

cānyǐn ānpái de yuánzé:
餐饮安排的原则：
Principles of catering arrangement:

① xiàng yóukè gōngkāi jiùcān biāozhǔn
  向游客公开就餐标准
  Publicizing dining standards to tourists

② quèbǎo shànshí zhìliàng
  确保膳食质量
  Ensuring dietary quality

③ dǎoyóu yào qǐdào jiǎngjiě、bǎozhàng de zuòyòng
  导游要起到讲解、保障的作用
  Tour guides should play a role in providing explanation and assurance.

cānyǐn fúwù
餐饮服务
Catering Service

导游工作用语：

Shǒuxiān hěn huānyíng dàjiā láidào Jiǎnpǔzhài, wǒ shì jīntiān dàilǐng dàjiā de dǎoyóu.
首先很欢迎大家来到柬埔寨，我是今天带领大家的导游。

Jīntiān wǒmen jiāng pǐncháng dào Jiǎnpǔzhài de tèsè fēngwèi měishí. Jiǎnpǔzhài rén de zhǔshí shì
今天我们将品尝到柬埔寨的特色风味美食。柬埔寨人的主食是

大米，副食以鱼虾、生菜和凉拌菜为主。其中，最具风味特色的
是"凉拌菜"，把新鲜的蔬菜洗干净后，放入葱、姜、蒜、辣椒、
椰汁等佐料调制而成，酸咸适度，香辣可口。下面请大家品尝
这一特色美食吧。

Useful expressions for tour guides:
　　First of all, welcome to Cambodia. I'm your tour guide. Today we will taste the special cuisine of Cambodia. The staple food of Cambodians is rice, and the main accompaniments includes fish shrimp, lettuce and cold dishes. Among them, the best-known local delicacy is the "cold dishes". After the fresh vegetables are washed, shallot, ginger, garlic, pepper, coconut milk and other seasonings are added. It is moderately sour, salty, spicy and delicious. Now please enjoy this hearty meal.

我的工作：
今天你将接待一个来自中国的旅游团，共有20人。他们将参观独立纪念碑，并在周边用餐。现在请听一段有关独立纪念碑的解说词，并选择正确的答案填在横线上。

My job:
You are going to receive a group of 20 tourists from China today. They are going to visit the Independence Monument. Now listen to a commentary of the Independence Monument and choose the correct answers to fill in the blanks.

中文 + 景点导游

独立纪念碑是金边的一座_____①_____，位处诺罗敦大道和西哈努克大道的交会处，靠近_____②_____，伫立在BKK西南区的_____③_____中，为纪念1953年11月9日柬埔寨摆脱法国殖民统治，获得完全独立而建。纪念碑于1958年3月落成，高37米，共7层，上有_____④_____（柬埔寨文化象征）100条。每年_____⑤_____时，柬埔寨国王或国王代表都要在此举行隆重的庆典。来访的外国元首也多到这里献花圈。

As a monument in Phnom Penh, the Independence Monument is located at the intersection of Norodom Boulevard and Sihanouk Boulevard, close to the Mekong River and standing in the big ring in the southwest of BKK. It was built to commemorate Cambodia's full independence from French colonial rule on November 9, 1953. Completed in March 1958, it is 37 meters high and has seven stories, with 100 snake gods (symbols of Cambodian culture) on it. On the Independence Day every year, the king of Cambodia or the king's representative holds a grand celebration here, and visiting foreign heads also come here to lay a wreath.

A. 大圆环　　B. 蛇神　　C. 独立节　　D. 湄公河　　E. 纪念碑

① _____　② _____　③ _____　④ _____　⑤ _____

工作模块三　Working Module 3

景区商业服务、住宿服务。Scenic spot commercial service and accommodation service.

```
liǎojiě yóukè zhùsù xūqiú
了解游客住宿需求
Understand the accommodation needs of tourists
        ↓
tíchū zhùsù biāozhǔn hé dìdiǎn jiànyì
提出住宿标准和地点建议
Propose accommodation standards and locations
        ↓
jǐngqū zhùsù ānquán tíshì
景区住宿安全提示
Tips for safe accommodation in scenic spots
```

zhùsù biāozhǔn	zhùsù dìdiǎn	tèshū yāoqiú
住宿标准	住宿地点	特殊要求
Accommodation standard	Accommodation location	Special needs

导游住宿接待工作流程：

- Zài dǐdá fàndiàn de tú zhōng xiàng yóukè jiǎndān jièshào fàndiàn qíngkuàng jí zhù diàn de yǒuguān
在抵达饭店的途中向游客简单介绍饭店情况及住店的有关

- zhùyì shìxiàng;
  注意事项;

- lǚyóutuán dǐdá fàndiàn hòu, hé lǐngduì yǐndǎo yóukè dào zhǐdìng dìdiǎn bànlǐ rù diàn shǒuxù;
  旅游团抵达饭店后，和领队引导游客到指定地点办理入店手续；

- yóukè jìnrù fángjiān zhīqián, xiàng yóukè jièshào fàndiàn nèi jiùcān xíngshì、dìdiǎn、shíjiān, bìng gàozhī yǒuguān huódòng de shíjiān ānpái;
  游客进入房间之前，向游客介绍饭店内就餐形式、地点、时间，并告知有关活动的时间安排；

- děngdài xíngli sòngdá fàndiàn, fùzé héduì xíngli, dūcù xínglǐyuán jíshí jiāng xíngli sòng zhì yóukè fángjiān;
  等待行李送达饭店，负责核对行李，督促行李员及时将行李送至游客房间；

- zài jiéshù dàngtiān huódòng líkāi fàndiàn zhīqián, yǔ lǐngduì shāngdìng dì-èr tiān de jiàozǎo shíjiān bìng ānpái hǎo jiàozǎo fúwù.
  在结束当天活动离开饭店之前，与领队商定第二天的叫早时间并安排好叫早服务。

Procedures of tour guide's accommodation arrangement:

- On the way to the hotel, briefly introduce the hotel and relevant precautions for hotel accommodation to tourists;
- After the tourist group arrives at the hotel, work with the team leader to guide the tourists to the designated place for check-in;
- Before tourists enter their rooms, the tour guide shall introduce the dining form, place and time in the hotel to tourists, and inform them of the time of relevant activities;
- After the baggage has been delivered to the hotel, check the baggage and urge the bellboy to send the baggage to the tourists' rooms in time;
- Before leaving the hotel, agree with the team leader on the morning call time of the next day and arrange the morning call service.

我的工作：
今天你将接待一个来自中国的旅游团，共有10人。他们来柬埔寨度过5天的假期。请你根据他们各自的需求为他们推荐合适的住宿酒店。

My job:
You will receive a group of 10 tourists from China today. They will spend a five-day holiday in Cambodia. Please recommend suitable hotels for them according to their respective needs.

住宿安排 Accommodation arrangement

尊敬的游客：

　　根据大家自身的情况，我给大家列出了一些推荐入住的酒店，请自行斟酌选择。祝您入住愉快。

Dear visitors,

　　Based on your individual circumstances, I have listed some recommended hotels for you. Please take your choice. Have a nice stay.

yóukè xìngmíng 游客 姓名 Tourists' name	rénshù 人数 Number of people	jiǔdiàn dìdiǎn 酒店 地点 Hotel location	jiǔdiàn fángxíng 酒店 房型 Hotel room type	tèshū xūqiú 特殊 需求 Special needs

项目四　Item 4
其他辅助服务　Other Supporting Services

我的工作　My job

1. 规范与流程：学习景区其他辅助服务流程、规范和服务用语。
   Procedures and Specifications: Learning other supporting service procedures, specifications and service terms of the scenic spot.
2. 工作模块一：景区交通服务。
   Module 1: Scenic spot traffic service.
3. 工作模块二：景区安全服务。
   Module 2: Scenic spot security service.
4. 工作模块三：景区娱乐服务。
   Module 3: Scenic spot entertainment service.

流程与规范 Procedures and Specifications

看视频，了解景区其他辅助服务流程与规范，请判断下列服务属于哪个辅助服务流程。
Watch the video to understand the procedures and specifications of other supporting services in scenic spots. Please determine which supporting service procedures the following services fall under.

A. 给游客提供娱乐项目建议和参考，告知游客在进行相关娱乐项目时的安全隐患。
Provide entertainment suggestions and reference to tourists, and inform them of the potential safety hazards associated with the entertainment.

B. 为游客设计合适的景区游览线路，安排好景区游览车。
Design suitable tour routes for tourists and arrange sightseeing buses.

C. 提醒游客注意有关饮食安全、蚊虫叮咬导致的疾病（如登革热）等的预防。
Remind tourists to pay attention to food safety and take precautions against diseases caused by insect bites, such as dengue fever, etc.

我未来的工作 3
My Future Job

① quèrèn yóukè rénshù、niánlíng、cānguān jǐngqū
 确认 游客人数、年龄、参观景区
  shízhǎng děng xìnxī
  时长 等信息
Confirm the number of tourists, their ages, duration of visit, and other information.

② zhìdìng yóulǎn lùxiàn
 制订 游览路线
Plan the tour route.

③ yúlè xiàngmù jièshào hé jiànyì
 娱乐 项目 介绍和建议
Introduce and recommend items of entertainment.

④ ānquán tíxǐng
 安全提醒
Remind them to pay attention to safety.

⑤ jiéshù
 结束
The end

A. _____

B. _____

C. _____

工作模块一　　Working Module 1

景区交通服务。Scenic spot traffic service.

Zhìdìng yóulǎn lùxiàn:
制订 游览 路线：
Plan the tour route:

Quèrèn yóukè shùliàng;
❶ 确认 游客 数量；
Confirm the number of tourists;

liǎojiě yóukè niánlíng jí shēntǐ zhuàngkuàng;
❷ 了解 游客 年龄 及 身体 状况 ；
Get to know the ages and physical conditions of tourists;

liǎojiě yóuwán shícháng;
❸ 了解 游玩 时长；
Get to know the duration of their visit.

shèjì yóulǎn lùxiàn.
❹ 设计 游览 路线。
Design the tour route.

Jiāotōng ānpái:
交通 安排：
Transportation arrangement:

❶ Yùdìng jǐngqū yóulǎnchē;
预订 景区 游览车；
Book the sightseeing bus.

❷ gàozhī yóukè jǐngqū shàng-xià chē dìdiǎn.
告知 游客 景区 上 下 车 地点。
Inform tourists of the pick-up and drop-off points in the scenic spot.

我的工作：
今天你将接待一个来自中国的旅游团，共有20人。他们将参观钟形塔和滨江公园。现在请你确认下旅行团的情况，并设计几条合适的参观路线。

My job:
You will receive a group of 20 tourists from China today. They will visit Wat Phnom and the Riverside Park. Please confirm the information of the tour group and design several suitable tour routes.

cānguān lùxiàn
参观 路线
Tour routes

cānguān lùxiàn 参观路线 Tour routes	cānguān shícháng 参观 时长 Duration of visit	lùxiàn tèsè 路线特色 Features of the route	shìhé rénqún 适合人群 Target tourists	jiāotōng qíngkuàng 交通 情况 Transportation

工作模块二 Working Module 2

景区安全服务。Scenic spot security service.

Yóukè huànbìng yùfáng:
游客 患病 预防：
Prevention of illness among tourists:

① Xiángxì liǎojiě tuánduì qíngkuàng;
详细了解团队情况；
Get to know the information of the group in detail.

② hélǐ ānpái huódòng;
合理安排活动；
Arrange activities reasonably.

③ tíxǐng yóukè zhùyì yǐnshí wèishēng;
提醒游客注意饮食卫生；
Remind visitors to pay attention to dietary hygiene.

④ jíshí bàogào tiānqì biànhuà;
及时报告天气变化；
Report weather changes in a timely manner.

⑤ tíxǐng yóukè zì bèi chángyòngyào.
提醒游客自备常用药。
Remind visitors to bring their own commonly used medicines.

Yóukè zài lǚtú zhōng huò yóulǎn zhōng huàn yìbān jíbìng huò gǎndào búshì:
游客在旅途中或游览中患一般疾病或感到不适：
When a tourist develops a common disease or feels uncomfortable during the journey or visiting:

① Ruò zhèngzhuàng jiào qīng, duō jiā guānxīn, zhàogù qí zuò zài qiánpái jiào shūfu de zuòwèi shang;
若症状较轻，多加关心，照顾其坐在前排较舒服的座位上；
If the symptoms are mild, pay more attention to the tourist and arrange him/her to sit in the front row.

② cānguān yóulǎn shí, shíkè guānchá yóukè de shéntài、qìsè, bìyào shí yě kě qǐng jǐngqū yīwù rényuán bāngmáng;
参观游览时，时刻观察游客的神态、气色，必要时也可请景区医务人员帮忙；
During the visit, always observe the tourist's bearing and complexion, and ask the medical staff of the scenic spot for help if necessary.

③ ruò bìngqíng jiào zhòng, péitóng yóukè qiánwǎng yīyuàn jiùyī.
若病情较重，陪同游客前往医院就医。
In case of a serious illness, accompany the tourist to the hospital for medical treatment.

我未来的工作 / My Future Job

导游工作用语：

Huānyíng dàjiā láidào Jiǎnpǔzhài, wǒ shì jīntiān dàilǐng dàjiā de dǎoyóu. Xiàmiàn wǒ xiǎng
欢迎大家来到柬埔寨，我是今天带领大家的导游。下面我想

tíxǐng dàjiā jǐ diǎn ānquán zhùyì shìxiàng, xīwàng wǒmen yōngyǒu yí gè ānquán yúkuài de lǚchéng.
提醒大家几点安全注意事项，希望我们拥有一个安全愉快的旅程。

Shǒuxiān qǐng dàjiā yángé ànzhào lǚxíngshè de ānpái dào zhǐdìng cāntīng yòngcān; búyào bàoyǐn-
首先请大家严格按照旅行社的安排到指定餐厅用餐；不要暴饮

-bàoshí, yǐmiǎn shuǐtǔ bùfú yǐnqǐ fùxiè. Qícì qǐng dàjiā zhùyì fánghù, bìmiǎn wénchóng
暴食，以免水土不服引起腹泻。其次请大家注意防护，避免蚊虫

dīngyǎo, yǐmiǎn gǎnrǎn dēnggérè. Qǐng dàjiā zì bèi fáng fùxiè, guòmǐn, gǎnmào děng cháng
叮咬，以免感染登革热。请大家自备防腹泻、过敏、感冒等常

yòng yàopǐn, búyào qīngyì jiāng zìjǐ de yào gěi qítā yóukè fúyòng. Rú què yǒu xūyào,
用药品，不要轻易将自己的药给其他游客服用。如确有需要，

kě bōdǎ Jiǎnpǔzhài yīliáo jíjiù diànhuà 119.
可拨打柬埔寨医疗急救电话119。

Useful expressions for tour guides:

Welcome to Cambodia. I am your tour guide today. Now I would like to remind you of some safety precautions and hope that we can have a safe and pleasant journey. Firstly, please dine at the designated restaurant by following the travel agency's arrangement strictly; do not overeat to avoid diarrhea caused by unacclimatization. Secondly, please protect yourself from insect bites to prevent the risk of catching dengue fever. Please bring some commonly used medicines to prevent diarrhea, allergies, colds, etc. for yourselves. Do not easily share your medicine with other tourists. If necessary, call the emergency medical service in Cambodia: 119.

我的工作：

今天你要接待一个来自中国的旅游团，共有20人。他们将参观钟形塔。现在请听一段有关钟形塔的解说词，并选择正确的答案填在横线上。

My job:

You are going to receive a group of 20 tourists from China today. They are going to visit Wat Phnom. Now listen to a commentary of Wat Phnom and choose the correct answers to fill in the blanks.

中文＋景点导游

　　钟形塔又名塔山、_____，建于_____，后多次重建。最近一次重建是在1926年。钟形塔位于金边第96街与诺罗敦大道交界。资料记载，这是金边市区_____，站在山上可以鸟瞰整个_____。山脚下是一个圆形花园，是一处香烟缭绕、阴凉而安静的市民休憩场所。上山的入口处有两个石刻的_____。拾级而上，两旁的扶手是_____的怪鸟、狮子、佛像等。关于塔山寺还有一段动人的故事，相传14世纪一名叫"奔"的女子捡到一尊因发大水顺_____漂流至此的_____，便把佛像筑于小山上，修建_____来供奉它，并逐渐发展成_____的城镇。

> Wat Phnom, also known as Wat Penh, was built in 1373 and rebuilt several times with the latest one in 1926. It is located at the intersection of the 96th Street and Norodom Boulevard in Phnom Penh. According to the records, this is the highest point in Phnom Penh. Standing on the hill, you can get a bird's eye view of the whole city. At the foot of the hill is a circular garden, a shaded and quiet place for citizens to rest, immersed in incense smoke. The handrails on both sides of the steps are carved with elaborate strange birds, lions, Buddhas and so on. There is a touching story about Wat Phnom. Legend has it that in the 14th century, a woman named Penh picked up a Statue of Buddha drifting down the Mekong River because of a flood. She put the Statue on the hill and built a temple to worship it, and the place has gradually developed into a prosperous town.

3 我未来的工作 My Future Job

A. 金边市 Jīnbiān Shì
B. 塔山寺 Tǎshān Sì
C. 湄公河 Méigōng Hé
D. 1373年 1373 nián
E. 制高点 zhìgāodiǎn
F. 繁华 fánhuá
G. 精工细刻 jīnggōng xìkè
H. 庙宇 miàoyǔ
I. 佛像 fóxiàng
J. 七头蛇神 qītóushéshén

① _____ ② _____ ③ _____ ④ _____
⑤ _____ ⑥ _____ ⑦ _____ ⑧ _____
⑨ _____ ⑩ _____

工作模块三 Working Module 3

景区娱乐服务。Entertainment services at scenic spots.

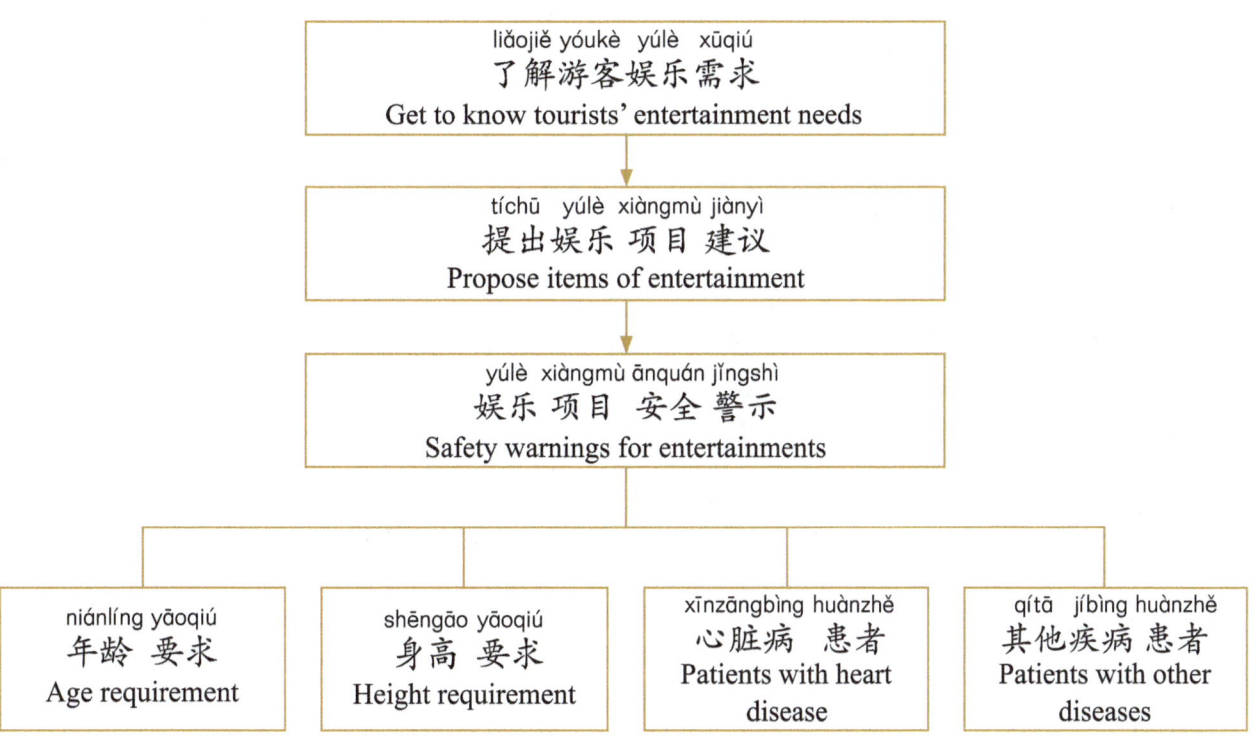

yúlè fúwù
娱乐 服务
Entertainment service

导游工作用语：

- Qǐng quèrèn zìjǐ de shēntǐ zhuàngtài, shēntǐ búshì huò yǒu xīnzāngbìng, gāoxuèyā, gānghē-guò jiǔ, tóuyūn-mùxuàn zhèxiē qíngkuàng jìnzhǐ tǐyàn wēixiǎn xiàngmù.
请确认自己的身体状态，身体不适或有心脏病、高血压、刚喝过酒、头晕目眩这些情况禁止体验危险项目。

- Zhèngquè zhuózhuāng, búyào chuān liányīqún、rénzìtuō、wú kòu dài píxié.
正确着装，不要穿连衣裙、人字拖、无扣带皮鞋。

- Zǐxì yuèdú yóukè xūzhī, liǎojiě guīzé, jìhǎo ānquán zhuāngzhì, bùdé zhōngtú jiěkāi shèbèi, bùdé xiédài yì rán yì bào wùpǐn rùchǎng.
仔细阅读游客须知，了解规则，系好安全装置，不得中途解开设备，不得携带易燃易爆物品入场。

- Yángé ànzhào zhǐshì jìnxíng cāozuò, fàngxia róngyì diàoluò de xiǎowùpǐn, rú yìngbì, yǎnjìng, shǒutíbāo, shǒujī.
严格按照指示进行操作，放下容易掉落的小物品，如硬币、眼镜、手提包、手机。

- Cānjiā shuǐshang xiàngmù shí, chuānhǎo jiùshēngyī; huáchuán, yóuyǒng, qiánshuǐ shí yídìng bù néng chāoyuè jǐngjièxiàn, yào yuǎnlí rénqún, yào tīngcóng jiùshēngyuán de zhǐhuī.
参加水上项目时，穿好救生衣；划船、游泳、潜水时一定不能超越警戒线，要远离人群，要听从救生员的指挥。

- Lǎorén hé xiǎoháir, yídìng yào liànglì'érxíng, yǐmiǎn zàochéng yìwài.
老人和小孩儿，一定要量力而行，以免造成意外。

- Chéngzuò lǎnchē、mótiānlún shí, qǐng jiāzhǎng zhàogù hǎo zìjǐ de xiǎoháir, tóu、shǒu búyào shēnchū chuāng wài.
乘坐缆车、摩天轮时，请家长照顾好自己的小孩儿，头、手不要伸出窗外。

我未来的工作
My Future Job — 3

Useful expressions for tour guides:
- Please confirm your physical status. You are prohibited from participating in dangerous activities if you feel uncomfortable, have heart disease or high blood pressure, have just drunk alcohol, or feel dizzy.
- Dress appropriately. Do not wear dresses, flip-flops, or leather shoes without buckles.
- Read the Notice to Visitors carefully to understand the rules, fasten the safety device, do not untie the device midway, and do not carry inflammables or explosives.
- Follow the instructions strictly and remove small items that are apt to fall, such as coins, glasses, handbags and mobile phones.
- Please wear life jackets for water entertainment activities, and do not go beyond the warning line when boating, swimming and diving. Stay away from other people, and follow the lifeguard's instructions.
- The elderly and children must act within their limits to avoid accidents.
- When taking a cable car or sky wheel, parents should take good care of their children, and do not put your head and hands out of the window.

我的工作：
今天你将接待一个来自中国的旅游团，共有 20 人。他们将参观钟形塔景点。游览结束后，游客还想去体验一些娱乐项目，请根据游客情况给他们推荐一些合适的娱乐项目。

My job:
You are going to receive a group of 20 tourists from China today. They will visit Wat Phnom. After the tour, they still want to participate in some entertainments. Please recommend some suitable entertainments to them.

娱乐项目建议　Recommended entertainments

尊敬的游客：
　　根据大家自身的情况，我给大家列出了一些娱乐项目建议，请自行斟酌选择。祝您玩得愉快！

Dear visitors,
　　Based on your individual circumstances, I have listed some recommended entertainments for you. Please make your own choice. Have a good time.

yóukè 游客	cónglín fēiyuè 丛林飞跃 The jungle leap	jiǎnshì ànmó 柬式按摩 Cambodia massage	rèqìqiú 热气球 Hot air balloon	qiánshuǐ 潜水 Diving
yóukè　1~4 游客 1~4				
yóukè　5~8 游客 5~8				

yóukè 游客	cónglín fēiyuè 丛林飞跃 The jungle leap	jiǎnshì ànmó 柬式按摩 Cambodia massage	rèqìqiú 热气球 Hot air balloon	qiánshuǐ 潜水 Diving
yóukè 9~12 游客 9～12				
yóukè 13~16 游客 13～16				
yóukè 17~20 游客 17～20				

项目五　Item 5
景点导游词 Tour Commentaries at Scenic Spots

我的工作　My job

1. 规范与流程：学习导游词的基本构成。
   Procedures and Specifications: Learning the basic composition of tour guide commentaries.
2. 工作模块一：导游词前言部分的作用及构成。
   Module 1: The function and composition of opening remarks.
3. 工作模块二：导游词总述部分的作用及构成。
   Module 2: The function and composition of general introduction.
4. 工作模块三：导游词分述部分的作用及构成。
   Module 3: The function and composition of detailed introduction.
5. 工作模块四：导游词结尾部分的作用及构成。
   module 4: The function and composition of ending part.

我未来的工作
My Future Job

3

流程与规范　Procedures and Specifications

看视频，了解景点导游词的基本构成，请将下列打乱顺序的金边王宫的导游词重新排序。

Watch the video to understand the basic composition of tour guide commentaries. Please re-sequence the following tour guide commentary of the Royal Palace of Phnom Penh.

liúchéng yǔ guīfàn
流 程 与 规 范
Procedures and Specifications

A. Hǎo le, wǒ de jièshào dào zhèlǐ jiù jiéshù le, shèngxià de shíjiān jiù yóu gèwèi ānpái le, xièxie dàjiā!
好了，我的介绍到这里就结束了，剩下的时间就由各位安排了，谢谢大家！
OK. That's the end of my introduction, and the rest of the time is yours. Thank you!

B. Gōngyuán 1434 nián Jiǎnpǔzhài guówáng Pénghēi'ā·Yàtè qiāndū Jīnbiān hòu, jí zài Jīnbiān xiūjiànle wánggōng. Zuòluò yú Jīnbiān dōngmiàn, miànduì Méigōng Hé、Dònglǐsà Hé、Bāshā Hé jiāohuì ér xíngchéng de Sìbì Wān, shǔyú diǎnxíng de gāomiánshì jiànzhù. Jiànzhù de wūdǐng zhōngyāng dōu yǒu gāogāo de jiāntǎ, wūjǐ liǎng duān jiānjiān qiàoqǐ, zàoxíng měiguān, jīnbì-huīhuáng. Cóng kōngzhōng fǔkàn, wánggōng yí piàn

公元1434年柬埔寨国王蓬黑阿·亚特迁都金边后，即在金边修建了王宫。坐落于金边东面，面对湄公河、洞里萨河、巴沙河交汇而形成的四臂湾，属于典型的高棉式建筑。建筑的屋顶中央都有高高的尖塔，屋脊两端尖尖翘起，造型美观，金碧辉煌。从空中俯瞰，王宫一片

129

中文+景点导游

jīnguāng shǎnshuò, géwài yǐnrén zhǔmù.
金光 闪烁，格外 引人 瞩目。

The Royal Palace of Phnom Penh was built in 1434 after Ponheia Yat, King of Cambodia, moved the capital to Phnom Penh. It is located in the east of the city, facing the Four Arms Bay where the Mekong River, Tonle Sap River and Bassac River converge. It is a typical Khmer architecture, with high spires in the central roof and two ends of the ridge pointed upward. Seen from above, the Palace is attractive, splendid, magnificent, and very noticeable.

Gèwèi xiānsheng、nǚshì, nǐmen hǎo! Huānyíng dàjiā lái cānguān Jiǎnpǔzhài Jīnbiān Wánggōng. Wǒ jiào
C. 各位 先生、女士，你们好！欢迎 大家 来 参观 柬埔寨 金边 王宫。我 叫
Xiǎo'ài, hěn róngxìng gěi nǐmen dāng dǎoyóu, yuàn nǐmen yǒu gè yúkuài de lǚchéng.
小爱，很 荣幸 给 你们 当 导游，愿 你们 有 个 愉快 的 旅程。

Hello, ladies and gentlemen! Welcome to the Royal Palace of Phnom Penh in Cambodia. I am Xiao Ai and very honored to be your tour guide. I wish you a happy journey.

Jīnbiān Wánggōng, shì Jiǎnpǔzhài Wángguó céngjīng de quánlì xiàngzhēng, céngjīng de huángjiā zhùsuǒ.
D. 金边 王宫，是 柬埔寨 王国 曾经 的 权力 象征， 曾经 的 皇家 住所。

The Royal Palace of Phnom Penh was once the royal residence, and the symbol of power of the Kingdom of Cambodia.

❶ _____ ➡ ❷ _____ ➡ ❸ _____ ➡ ❹ _____

工作模块一　Working Module 1

导游词前言部分的作用及构成。The function and composition of tour commentary's opening remarks.

dǎoyóucí qiányán
导游词前言
Tour Commentary's Opening Remarks

我未来的工作 3
My Future Job

Dǎoyóucí qiányán bùfen de zuòyòng:
导游词前言部分的作用：
Function of Tour Commentary's Opening Remarks:

① lājìn dǎoyóu yǔ yóukè de jùlí
拉近导游与游客的距离
To bring the tour guide and travelers closer

② yǐnqǐ yóukè duì rénshēn hé cáiwù ānquán de zhòngshì
引起游客对人身和财物安全的重视
To draw travelers' attention to their personal and property safety

③ kāiqǐ yúkuài de lǚchéng
开启愉快的旅程
To start a happy journey

Dǎoyóucí qiányán bùfen de gòuchéng:
导游词前言部分的构成：
Composition of Tour Commentary's Opening Remarks:

① huānyíngcí
欢迎辞
Welcoming speech

② zìwǒ jièshào
自我介绍
Self-introduction

③ ānquán tíxǐng
安全提醒
Safety tips

④ zhùyì shìxiàng tíxǐng
注意事项提醒
Reminders

⑤ měihǎo zhùyuàn
美好祝愿
Best wishes

导游词前言部分范例：

Huānyíng dàjiā lái Jiǎnpǔzhài lǚyóu, wǒ shì jīntiān dàilǐng dàjiā de dǎoyóu Xiǎo'ài, fēicháng
欢迎大家来柬埔寨旅游，我是今天带领大家的导游小爱，非常

róngxìng néng wèi dàjiā tígōng dǎoyóu fúwù. Wǒmen cóng zhèlǐ chūfā dào Zhōngxíng Tǎ jǐngdiǎn
荣幸能为大家提供导游服务。我们从这里出发到钟形塔景点

大概需要两个小时，马上要驶入高速，我想强调一下儿安全问题。请大家不要在车内随意走动，并扶好自己的扶手。保持车内环境卫生，垃圾丢在垃圾袋里。不要将手臂和头伸到窗外。另外，请大家在参观时注意财物安全，包不离身。自由活动时请带好联系卡，万一不小心走丢，可以及时联系。祝愿大家旅途愉快！

谢谢各位！

Examples of Opening Remarks:

Welcome to Cambodia! I am Xiao Ai, your tour guide, and I feel very honored to serve you. It will take about two hours to go from here to Wat Phnom. Before getting on the highway, I would like to draw your attention to your safety. Please do not walk around in the bus, and hold the handrail. Keep the bus clean, and put rubbish in the rubbish bag. Do not put your head and hands out of the window. In addition, during the visit, pay attention to the safety of your belongings, and keep an eye on your bags. During the free time, bring the contact card with you, so that you can contact me if you get lost. Wish you a pleasant journey! Thank you!

我的工作：

今天你将接待一个来自中国的旅游团，共有20人。他们将参观钟形塔。请你听听导游词前言部分的注意事项，并回答问题。

My job:

You will receive a group of 20 tourists from China today. They will visit Wat Phnom. Please listen to the points for attention in the tour commentary's opening remarks, and answer the following questions.

① 为什么旅行途中尽量不要流血？

Why do tourists try not to bleed during the journey?

_____

② 为什么不要摸当地人的头？

Why can't tourists touch local people's head?

_____

我未来的工作
My Future Job

Wèi shénme yào pēn fángwénshuǐ?
❸ 为什么要喷防蚊水?
Why do tourists need to spray the mosquito-repellent on their bodies?

_____.

Wèi shénme yào gēn tuán yìqǐ zǒu?
❹ 为什么要跟团一起走?
Why can't tourists leave the tour group?

_____.

工作模块二 Working Module 2

导游词总述部分的作用及构成。 The functions and compositions of tour commentary's general introduction.

Dǎoyóucí zǒngshù bùfen de zuòyòng:
导游词总述部分的作用:
Functions of Tour Commentary's General Introduction:

yǐnqǐ yóukè de xìngqù
❶ 引起游客的兴趣
To attract tourists' interest

wèi zhīhòu de jiǎngjiě dǎxià liánghǎo de jīchǔ
❷ 为之后的讲解打下良好的基础
To lay a solid foundation for the subsequent detailed introduction

Dǎoyóucí zǒngshù bùfen de gòuchéng:
导游词总述部分的构成:
Compositions of Tour Commentary's General Introduction:

jǐngdiǎn de dìwèi
❶ 景点的地位
Status of the scenic spot

jǐngdiǎn de lèixíng
❷ 景点的类型
Type of the scenic spot

jǐngdiǎn de tèdiǎn
❸ 景点的特点
Characteristics of the scenic spot

jǐngdiǎn de kàndiǎn
❹ 景点的看点
Highlights of the scenic spot

导游词总述部分范例:

Wúgē Kū yòu chēng Wúgē Miào, wèiyú Jiǎnpǔzhài de xīnán. Tā shì mùqián Wúgē gǔjì lǐ-
吴哥窟又称吴哥庙,位于柬埔寨的西南。它是目前吴哥古迹里

miàn bǎocún zuì wánhǎo de jiànzhù, yīn qí jiànzhù gòuzào hóngwěi jīngzhì ér wénmíng yú shì. Tā
面保存最完好的建筑,因其建筑构造宏伟精致而闻名于世。它

中文 + 景点导游

shì shìjiè shàng zuì dà de sìmiào. Liánhéguó Jiào-Kē-Wén Zǔzhī Shìjiè Yíchǎn Wěiyuánhuì yǐjīng
是世界上最大的寺庙。联合国教科文组织世界遗产委员会已经

jiāng zhěnggè Wúgē gǔjì liè wéi shìjiè wénhuà yíchǎn.
将整个吴哥古迹列为世界文化遗产。

Examples of Tour Commentary's General Introduction

Also known as Angkor Temple, Angkor Wat is located in the northwest of Cambodia. As the best preserved architecture in the historical sites in Angkor, it is known for its magnificent and exquisite architectural construction. It is the largest temple in the world. The whole Angkor site has been listed as the world cultural heritage site by the World Heritage Committee of UNESCO.

我的工作：

今天你要接待一个来自中国的旅游团，共有 20 人。他们将参观独立纪念碑。现在请听有关独立纪念碑解说词的总述部分，并选择正确的答案填在横线上。

My job:

You are going to receive a group of 20 tourists from China today. They are going to visit the Independence Monument. Now listen to the commentary's general introduction to the Independence Monument, and choose the correct answers to fill in the blanks.

Dúlì Jìniànbēi
独立纪念碑
Independence Monument

Dúlì Jìniànbēi wèiyú ___❶___ hé ___❷___ jiāochāchù, jìniàn ___❸___
独立纪念碑位于_____和_____交叉处，纪念_____

11 yuè 9 rì Jiǎnpǔzhài bǎituō ___❹___ zhímíntǒngzhì, wánquán dúlì ér jiàn. ___❺___
11月9日柬埔寨摆脱_____殖民统治，完全独立而建。_____

3 yuè luòchéng, ___❻___ , ___❼___ , yǒu shéshén Jiǎnpǔzhài wénhuà xiàngzhēng
3月落成，_____，_____，有蛇神（柬埔寨文化象征）

我未来的工作
My Future Job

_____⑧条。每年独立节时，柬埔寨国王或国王代表都要在此举行隆重的_____⑨。来访的外国_____⑩也多到这里献_____⑪。

> Located at the intersection of Norodom Boulevard and SihanouK Boulevard, the Independence Monument was built to commemorate Cambodia's full independence from French colonial rule on Nov. 9,1953. Completed in March, 1958, it is 37 meters high and has 7 stories, with 100 snake gods on it. On the Independence Day every year, the King of Cambodia or the king's representative holds a grand ceremony here, and the visiting foreign heads also come here to lay wreaths.

A. 法国 France
B. 7 层 7 stories
C. 100 条 100
D. 1958 年 1958
E. 西哈努克大道 Sihanouk Blvd
F. 37 米 37 meters
G. 庆典 celebration
H. 元首 head of a state
I. 诺罗敦大道 Norodom Blvd
J. 1953 年 1953
K. 花圈 wreath

① _____ ② _____ ③ _____ ④ _____
⑤ _____ ⑥ _____ ⑦ _____ ⑧ _____

135

⑨ _____ ⑩ _____ ⑪ _____

工作模块三 Working Module 3

导游词分述部分的作用及构成。The functions and compositions of the tour commentary's detailed introduction.

Dǎoyóucí fēnshù bùfen de zuòyòng:
导游词分述部分的 作用:
Functions of Tour Commentary's Detailed Introduction:

① jīfā yóukè de hǎoqíxīn
激发游客的好奇心
To stimulate tourists' curiosity

② zēngjiā yóukè de zhīshi jīlěi
增加游客的知识积累
To increase tourist' stock of knowledge

③ fēngfù yóukè de jīngshén shìjiè
丰富游客的精神世界
To enrich tourists' spiritual world

Dǎoyóucí fēnshù bùfen de gòuchéng:
导游词分述部分的 构成:
Compositions of the Tour Commentary's Detailed Introduction:

① jǐngdiǎn de lìshǐ
景点的历史
History of the scenic spot

② jǐngdiǎn de bèijǐng
景点的背景
Background of the scenic spot

③ xiāngguān de rénwù
相关的人物
Figures related to the scenic spot

④ jǐngdiǎn xiāngguān de shìjiàn (rú shénhuà gùshi děng)
景点 相关 的事件(如神话故事等)
Events related to the scenic spot (such as fairy tales)

我未来的工作
My Future Job

导游词分述部分范例（一）：

看，这就是鼎鼎有名的塔普隆寺，塔普隆寺已有近900年的历史了。整个寺庙被原始森林包围，粗壮的树干把墙都穿破了。动物也非常奇特，在草丛中随处可见蚂蚁一样小的青蛙。游客们请看，最神奇的是在树洞中可以见到一个跳舞的仙女，真是大自然的神来之笔！游客们别看塔普隆寺这么偏僻，这可是大片儿的拍摄地，什么《生化危机》《古墓丽影》《花样年华》等等，都是在这里拍摄的。你如果有心事和烦恼都可以跟树洞说。大家可以在这边合影留念。

Look! This is the famous Ta Prohm, with a history of nearly 900 years. The whole temple is enveloped by the virgin forest, and the thick trunks of the trees have broken through the walls. The animals here are very special, and you can find frogs as small as ants in the grass. The most fantastic thing is that you can find a dancing fairy in the tree hole, which is definitely a stroke of genius of nature. Though Ta Prohm is out of the way, it is the shooting place of many blockbusters, such as *Resident Evil*, *Tomb Raider*, *In the Mood for Love* and so on. It is said that if you have any worries or troubles, you can talk to the tree hole. You can take pictures here.

导游词分述部分范例（二）：

看，这就是美丽的女王宫，这里所有的壁画都是用红砖头精心雕刻而成。大家请往前走，大家请看，这是一个怪物在吃自己。让我来讲个有趣的故事吧：以前有一个神叫时间神，他非常胖，胃口特别大，把世界上的食物全部都吃完了，但是他觉得还是很饿，就去找毗湿奴神，毗湿奴神一听非常生气，说你这么胖，不如把你自己的肉吃了吧！时间神一听就开始吃自己，就把自己吃死了。毗湿奴神一听非常伤心，于是上天让天神把时间神又复活了。

……

Look! This is the beautiful Banteay Srei. The frescos here are all carved from red bricks. Go forward and you can find a monster who is eating himself! Let me tell an interesting story. Long long ago, there was a God named the God of Time. He was very fat and had a gigantic appetite. As a result, he ate up all food in the world, but still felt hungry. So he went to Lord Vishnu for advice. After hearing his story, Lord Vishnu was very angry and asked, "Why don't you eat yourself since you are so fat?" Guess what? The God of Time did begin to eat himself and died in the end! After hearing of his death, Lord Vishnu was very sad, and begged the supreme God to bring him back to life.

3 我未来的工作
My Future Job

我的工作：

今天你将接待一个来自中国的旅游团，共有20人。他们将参观吴哥窟。游览前，请听一段关于做好导游词分述部分讲解的介绍，然后判断下面的做法是否正确，正确的打√。

My job:

You are going to receive a group of 20 tourists from China today. They will visit Angkor Wat. Please listen to an introduction to the detailed introduction part, and determine whether the following practices are correct or not. Tick the correct ones.

( ) 1. 为了多介绍一些景点，每一个景点的讲解都蜻蜓点水带过。

To introduce more scenic spots, touch on every scenic spot without interpreting them in detail.

( ) 2. 对于景点相关的历史、人物、事件，直接从手机上下载，读给游客听。

Download the history, figures and events related to the scenic spot from the mobile and read them to the tourists.

( ) 3. 对于不了解的东西，可机智地回避，绝不可胡编乱造、胡说八道。

Avoid the details you are not sure about cleverly, but do not make up stories or talk nonsense.

( ) 4. 为了显示自己的语言水平，用书面语和长句子介绍景点。

To show off language proficiency, introduce the scenic spot with written words and long sentences.

( ) 5. 因文化差异而容易使游客产生不适或误解的神话故事，景点介绍时应尽量避免。

Try to avoid the fairy tales which are likely to make tourists uncomfortable or lead to misunderstanding due to cultural differences.

( ) 6. 为保持和游客良好的关系，在禁止拍照、抚摸的地方拍照和抚摸文物时，保持沉默。

To keep a good relationship with the tourists, keep silent when the tourists take photos or touch cultural relics in areas where photographing or touching is prohibited.

工作模块四　Working Module 4

导游词结尾部分的作用及构成。The function and composition of ending part.

Dǎoyóucí jiéwěi bùfen de zuòyòng:
导游词结尾部分的作用：
Functions of Tour Commentary's End:

① zǒngjié 总结　Summary
② gōutōng 沟通　Communication
③ dáchéng liàngjiě 达成 谅解　Mutual understanding
④ zàicì hézuò 再次合作　Cooperation again

Dǎoyóucí jiéwěi bùfen de gòuchéng:
导游词结尾部分的构成：
Compositions of the Tour Commentary's End:

① duì běn cì jiǎngjiě de zǒngjié 对本次讲解的总结　Summary of the commentary
② duì yóukè biǎoshì gǎnxiè 对游客表示感谢　Expressing gratitude to the tourists
③ biǎoshì xīwàng zàicì jiànmiàn de yuànwàng 表示希望再次见面的愿望　Expressing wishes to meet the tourists again
④ sòngshang zìjǐ měihǎo de zhùyuàn 送上自己美好的祝愿　Sending best wishes

---

导游词结尾部分范例

Wǒmen yì tiān de yóulǎn jiù yào jiéshù le, dànyuàn zhè cì cānguān néng gěi dàjiā liúxia
我们一天的游览就要结束了，但愿这次参观 能给大家留下

shēnkè de yìnxiàng. Fēicháng gǎnxiè dàjiā duì wǒ de xìnrèn, fúwù zhōng de bùzú zhī chù,
深刻的印象。非常感谢大家对我的信任，服务中的不足之处，

xīwàng dàjiā duōduō bāohán, duō tí bǎoguì yìjiàn. Huānyíng dàjiā xié jiārén hé péngyou zàicì
希望大家多多包涵，多提宝贵意见。欢迎大家携家人和朋友再次

lái zhèlǐ cānguān hé xiǎngshòu. Xièxie dàjiā, zàijiàn!
来这里参观和享受。谢谢大家，再见！

Examples of the Tour Commentary's End:

Our visit will soon come to an end and I do hope this tour will leave a deep impression on you. Thank you for your trust and understanding, and your advice will be highly appreciated. I hope to serve you, your family and friends here again. Thank you! Good bye!

我的工作：

今天你接待了一个来自中国的旅游团，共有20人。他们参观了滨江公园。游览结束前，你将送上你的告别语。请选出下面告别语的类型，并说一说、练一练。

My job:

You have received a group of 20 tourists from China today. They visited the Riverside Park. Before the end of the visit, you need to deliver your ending remarks. Please determine the types of the following ending remarks and practice them.

A. zhēngqiú yìjiànyǔ 征求意见语 — asking for opinions
B. zhìqiànyǔ 致歉语 — making an apology
C. xībiéyǔ 惜别语 — farewells
D. gǎnxièyǔ 感谢语 — thanks
E. zhùyuànyǔ 祝愿语 — best wishes

1. Mǎshàng jiù yào dào jiǔdiàn, yě yào hé dàjiā shuō zàijiàn le.
   马上就要到酒店，也要和大家说再见了。
   I have to say goodbye to you as we are arriving at the hotel.

2. Zài cǐ wǒ fēicháng gǎnxiè gè wèi péngyou duì wǒ gōngzuò de zhīchí, gǎnxiè dàjiā de pèihé.
   在此我非常感谢各位朋友对我工作的支持，感谢大家的配合。
   Thank you for your support and cooperation.

中文 + 景点导游

3. 在几天的游览过程中，如果有什么不足之处，还请多谅解。
   Zài jǐ tiān de yóulǎn guòchéng zhōng, rúguǒ yǒu shénme bùzú zhī chù, hái qǐng duō liàngjiě.
   Please excuse any shortcomings there may be during the journey.

4. 欢迎您对我的服务工作提出意见和建议。您的意见将是我努力的方向，您的建议将是我改进的目标。
   Huānyíng nín duì wǒ de fúwù gōngzuò tíchū yìjiàn hé jiànyì. Nín de yìjiàn jiāng shì wǒ nǔlì de fāngxiàng, nín de jiànyì jiāng shì wǒ gǎijìn de mùbiāo.
   Your comments and suggestions on my service will be highly appreciated. Your comments will guide my efforts and your suggestions will be my goal of improvement.

5. 希望能有机会再次为您服务。祝大家一路平安！
   Xīwàng néng yǒu jīhuì zàicì wéi nín fúwù. Zhù dàjiā yílù-píng'ān!
   I do hope I can serve you again and wish you a safe journey!

① _____ ② _____ ③ _____ ④ _____ ⑤ _____

4

Gōngzuòfáng shíxùn
工作坊实训
Practical Training at Workshops

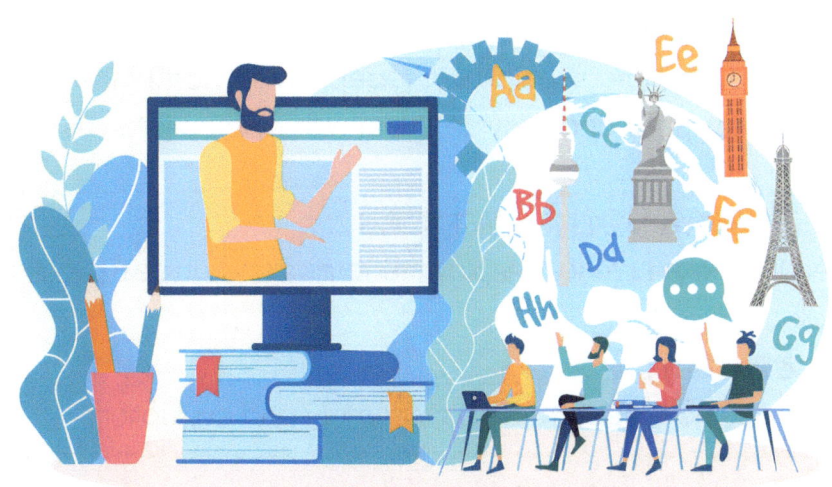

项目一　Item 1
景区接待实训　*Simulation of Reception at Scenic Spots*

实训目的：根据景区接待服务流程模拟景区接待服务。
Training Purpose: To simulate the scenic spot reception service according to the reception service procedures.
实训组织：每组3～5人。
Training organization: 3-5 persons per group.
实训内容：假设你是某景区的景区导游，景区接待处安排你明天接待来自中国江苏的贵宾一行10人游览，请做好景区接待服务工作。
Training content: Suppose you are a tour guide of a scenic spot. The reception office of the scenic spot has arranged for you to receive a group of 10 guests from Jiangsu, China tomorrow. Please ensure proper reception service.

实训步骤：

Training steps:

1. 老师将实训教室分成若干个虚拟的景区，用图片代表各个景点。

   The teacher divides the training classroom into several virtual scenic spots, and represents each scenic spot with a picture.

2. 将参加实训的学生分组，每组 3～5 人。

   Divide the trainees into groups of 3-5.

3. 带领学生在各个景点以对话的形式模拟景区接待服务，过程中给予学生适当帮助。

   Take students to simulate scenic spot reception service in the form of dialogues at various scenic spots, and provide them with appropriate assistance during the process.

4. 小组成员轮流扮演旅客和导游，练习并表演对话。

   Group members take turns to role-play the tourists and guides, practicing and acting out the dialogue.

5. 实训结束，老师总结评价。

   After the training, the teacher makes a summary and evaluation.

项目二　Item 2
景区解说实训　Simulation of Commentaries at Scenic Spots

实训目的：根据景区解说服务流程模拟景区解说服务。

Training Purpose: To simulate interpretation service in scenic spots according to interpretation service procedures.

实训组织：每组 3～5 人。

Training organization: 3-5 persons per group.

实训内容：假设你是某景区的景区导游，景区接待处安排你明天接待来自中国江苏的贵宾一行 10 人游览，请做好景区解说服务工作。

Training content: Suppose you are a tourist guide of a scenic spot. The reception office of the scenic spot has arranged for you to receive a group of 10 guests from Jiangsu, China tomorrow. Please provide excellent interpretation service.

实训步骤：

Training steps:

1. 将参加实训的学生分组，每组 3～5 人。

   Divide the trainees into groups of 3-5.

2. 带领学生以对话的形式分别模拟旅游景区环境解说、旅游吸引物解说和旅游管理解说，过程中给予学生适当帮助。
   Lead students to simulate scenic spot environmental interpretation, tourist attractions interpretation, and tourism management interpretation in the form of dialogues, and provide them with appropriate assistance during the process.
3. 小组成员轮流扮演游客和导游，练习并表演对话。
   Group members take turns to role play the tourists and guides, practicing and acting out the dialogue.
4. 实训结束，老师总结评价。
   After the training, the teacher makes a summary and evaluation.

项目三　Item 3
景区购物服务实训　Simulation of Shopping Service at Scenic Spots

实训目的：根据景区购物服务流程模拟景区购物服务。
Training purpose: To simulate the shopping service in scenic spots according to the shopping service procedures.

实训组织：每组3～5人。
Training organization: 3-5 people per group.

实训内容：假设你是某景区的景区导游，景区接待处安排你明天接待来自中国江苏的贵宾一行10人购物，请做好景区购物接待服务工作。
Training content: Suppose you are a tourist guide of a scenic spot. The reception office of the scenic spot has arranged for you to receive a group of 10 guests from Jiangsu, China tomorrow. Please ensure good service for shopping.

实训步骤：
Training steps:

1. 老师将实训教室分成若干个虚拟的景区购物店，用图片代表各个购物类别。
   The teacher divides the training classroom into several virtual shops in a scenic spot, and represents various goods with pictures.
2. 将参加实训的学生分组，每组3～5人。
   Divide the trainees into groups of 3-5.
3. 带领学生在各个景点以对话的形式模拟景区购物接待服务，过程中给予学生适当帮助。
   Take students to simulate shopping service in the form of dialogues at various spots, and provide them with appropriate assistance during the process.

4. 小组成员轮流扮演旅客和导游，练习并表演对话。
   Group members take turns to role-play the tourists and guides, practicing and acting out the dialogue.
5. 实训结束，老师总结评价。
   After the training, the teacher makes a summary and evaluation.

项目四　Item 4
其他辅助服务实训　Simulation of Other Supporting Service

实训目的：根据景区其他辅助服务流程模拟景区其他辅助服务。
Training Purpose: To simulate other supporting services in scenic spots according to other supporting service procedures.

实训组织：每组3～5人。
Training organization: 3-5 persons per group.

实训内容：假设你是某景区的景区导游，景区接待处安排你明天接待来自中国江苏的贵宾一行10人游览，请做好景区交通、安全和娱乐服务工作。
Training content: Suppose you are a tourist guide of a scenic spot. The reception office of the scenic spot has arranged for you to receive a group of 10 guests from Jiangsu, China tomorrow. Please ensure the proper provision of the transportation, safety and entertainment service.

实训步骤：
Training steps:

1. 将参加实训的学生分组，每组3～5人。
   Divide the trainees into groups of 3-5.
2. 带领学生以对话的形式分别模拟景区交通、安全和娱乐服务，过程中给予学生适当帮助。
   Take students to simulate the transportation, safety and entertainment service in the form of dialogues, and provide them with appropriate assistance during the process.
3. 小组成员轮流扮演游客和导游，练习并表演对话。
   Group members take turns to role-play the tourists and guides, practicing and acting out the dialogue.
4. 实训结束，老师总结评价。
   After the training, the teacher makes a summary and evaluation.

项目五　Item 5
景点导游词讲解实训　Simulation of Delivering Tour Commentaries

实训目的：景点导游词讲解模拟。
Training Purpose: To simulate the delivery of tour commentaries.

实训组织：每组 3～5 人。
Training organization: 3-5 persons per group.

实训内容：假设你是某景区的景区导游，景区接待处安排你明天接待来自中国江苏的贵宾一行 10 人游览，请做好景区景点的讲解工作。
Training content: Suppose you are a tourist guide of a scenic spot. The reception office of the scenic spot has arranged for you to receive a group of 10 guests from Jiangsu, China tomorrow. Please deliver outstanding interpretation of the scenic spot.

实训步骤：
Training steps:

1. 老师将实训教室分成若干个虚拟的景区，用图片代表各个景点。
   The teacher divides the training classroom into several virtual scenic spots, and represents each scenic spot with a picture.
2. 将参加实训的学生分组，每组 3～5 人。
   Divide the trainees into groups of 3-5.
3. 教师在各个景点模拟导游进行景点讲解。
   The teacher simulates the guide's interpretation of scenic spots.
4. 小组成员轮流扮演旅客和导游，练习各个景点的导游词。
   Group members take turns to role-play the tourists and guides, practicing and acting out the dialogue.
5. 实训结束，老师总结评价。
   After the training, the teacher makes a summary and evaluation.

附录　Appendixes

导游常用语 100 句
100 common expressions used by tour guides

1. 欢迎大家来到×××，我是今天带领大家的导游。
   Welcome to ×××. I'm your tour guide today.

2. 希望我们的服务能让您满意，祝您有一个轻松愉快的旅程！
   I hope you will be satisfied with our service and have a pleasant and relaxing trip!

3. 祝大家玩得愉快！
   Have a good time, everyone.

4. 入境前请您填写入境卡。
   Please fill in the arrival card before entering the country.

5. 红色通道也称"申报通道"，绿色通道也称"免税通道"或"无申报通道"。
   The red channel is also known as the "Goods to Declare Channel", and the green channel is also known as "Duty-Free Channel" or "Nothing-to-Declare Channel".

6. 安全检查的内容主要是检查旅客及其行李物品中是否携带枪支、弹药、易爆、腐蚀、有毒、放射性等危险物品。
   The main task of security check is to check whether passengers and their luggage carry arms and ammunition, explosives, corrosives, toxic and radioactive substances, and other dangerous articles.

7. 您先在这里填写姓名、出生地点和日期。
   First, fill in your name, place and date of birth here.

8. 请接下来填写国籍、护照号、航班号、来自何处、签证类型、签发地点。
   Next, please fill in your nationality, passport number, flight number, place of departure, visa type and place of issue.

9. 请最后填写入境目的、停留天数和居住的地址。
   Finally, please fill in the purpose of entry, length of stay and address of residence.

10. 您需要准备护照和签证。
    You need to prepare your passport and visa.

11. 现在是金边/雅加达/河内时间上午八点。
    It's 8 a.m. Phnom Penh / Jakarta / Hanoi Time.

12. ××在东七区。
    ×× is in GMT+7:00.

13. 北京在东八区。
    Beijing is in GMT+8:00.

14. ××和北京的时差是多少？
    What is the time difference between XX and Beijing?

15. 金边时间比北京时间慢一个小时。
    Phnom Penh Time is one hour behind Beijing Time.

16. 您已经穿越了国际日期变更线，使得时间不一样了。
    You have crossed the International Date Line, which makes the time different.

17. 时差反应指人们在乘飞机飞越不同时区后的疲劳感。
    The time difference, also known as jet lag, is the feeling of fatigue after a flight across different time zones.

18. 您经历国际时差会感觉不舒服吗？
    Do you feel uncomfortable with the international jet lag?

19. 下面这些方法能缓解时差带给您的不适感。
    Here are some ways to ease the discomfort of jet lag.

20. 如果国际时差给您的旅程带来不便，告诉我，我将尽全力帮您解决。
    If the international time difference brings you any inconvenience, please let me know and I will do my best to help you.

21. 本机场有三家运营商可供选择，Smart、Cellcard 和 Metfone。
    There are three operators to choose from at the airport, Smart, Cellcard and Metfone.

22. 请您出示您的护照给工作人员，选择流量套餐。
    Please show your passport to the staff and choose the data package.

23. 请选择您需要充值的金额，刷卡还是付现金？
    Please select the recharge amount. Would you like to pay by credit card or in cash?

24. 充值完成了，这是您的SIM卡，放在手机里就可以使用了。
    The recharge is completed. This is your SIM card. You can use your phone after inserting it into your mobile phone.

25. 您还可以租用便携的WIFI设备，也是可以上网的。
    You can also rent a portable WiFi device and surf the Internet.

26. 便携WIFI的租金是单价乘行程天数乘台数加押金。
    The rent of a portable WiFi is unit price × days of your travel × number of sets+ deposit.

27. 根据大家自身的情况，给大家列出了一些推荐入住的酒店，请自行斟酌选择。祝您入住愉快。
    Based on your individual circumstances, I have listed some recommended hotels for you. Please make a choice. Enjoy your stay.

28. 今晚我们将要入住的是位于……的×酒店，酒店为您提供了全程免费WIFI服务，可以时刻与好友保持联系。
    We will stay in × Hotel tonight. The hotel provides you with free WIFI service throughout the whole journey, so you can keep in touch with your friends all the time.

29. 网络信号覆盖酒店大堂、餐厅、泳池和行政酒廊等公共区域以及客房。
    The network signal covers public areas, such as the hotel lobby, restaurants, swimming pools and lounge, as well as guest rooms.

30. 您可以在酒店的任何位置畅快地使用WIFI网络。
    You can use WiFi network freely anywhere in the hotel.

31. 入住的客人可使用手机打开无线WIFI上网功能。
    Guests staying in the hotel can use their mobile phones to turn on WiFi network function.

32. 您可以连接名为"×××Hotel"的WiFi号。
    You can connect to the WiFi signal named "××× Hotel".

33. Nín jiēzhe zài tiàozhuǎn yèmiàn zhōng shūrù 6 hé bànlǐ rùzhù de fángkè xìngmíng, jí kě shǐyòng hùliánwǎng le.
您接着在 跳转 页面 中 输入6和办理入住的房客 姓名，即可使用 互联网 了。
Then enter 6 and the name of the guest who has checked in on the link page to use the Internet.

34. Chū-rù jiǔdiàn qǐng suíshǒu guānmén.
出入酒店 请 随手 关门。
Please close the door after you when entering and leaving the hotel.

35. Qǐngwù zài chuáng shang chōuyān.
请勿在 床 上 抽烟。
Do not smoke in bed.

36. Qǐng tīngcóng gōngzuò rényuán zhǐhuī, yǒuxù rùchǎng.
请 听从 工作 人员 指挥，有序入场。
Please follow the instructions of the staff and enter the site in an orderly manner.

37. Qǐngwù xiédài yìrán、yìbào、yǒudú wùpǐn.
请勿携带易燃、易爆、有毒物品。
Do not carry flammable, explosive or toxic items.

38. Fēijī shēng-jiàng shí, qǐngwù shǐyòng diànzǐ chǎnpǐn.
飞机 升降 时，请勿 使用 电子 产品。
Do not use electronic devices while the aircraft is taking off and landing.

39. Qǐng láojì jiùshēngyī de shǐyòng fāngfǎ.
请牢记 救生衣 的 使用 方法。
Please keep in mind how to use your life jacket.

40. Qǐng jìzhù mièhuǒqì de wèizhì.
请记住 灭火器的 位置。
Please remember the location of fire extinguishers.

41. Qǐng jìzhù jíhé shíjiān hé dìdiǎn.
请记住 集合 时间 和 地点。
Please remember the gathering time and place.

42. Qǐng búyào yōngdǔ zài rùkǒu chù.
请不要 拥堵 在入口处。
Please don't crowd at the entrance.

43. Nín hǎo, huānyíng guānglín. Yǒu shénme kěyǐ wéi nín xiàoláo de, fūrén?
您好，欢迎 光临。有什么可以为您效劳的，夫人？
Hello, welcome to xxx. What can I do for you, madam?

44. Nà wǒ jiànyì nín kěyǐ mǎi xiē sīchóu huòzhě xiǎoxíng de mùdiāo.
那我建议您可以买些丝绸 或者 小型 的木雕。
Then I suggest you to buy some silk or small wood carvings.

45. Zhèxiē gōngyìpǐn bùjǐn měiguān、shíyòng, yě biànyú xiédài, kěyǐ zuòwéi lǐpǐn zèngsòng gěi qīnpéng-hǎoyǒu.
这些 工艺品 不仅美观、实用，也便于携带，可以作为礼品 赠送 给 亲朋 好友。
These handicrafts are not only beautiful and practical, but are also easy to carry. They can be presented to relatives and friends as gifts.

46. Zhè shì nín de zhǎolíng, shāo děng, wǒ bāng nín bǎ tā bāo qǐlai.
这是您的 找零， 稍 等，我帮您把它包起来。
Here's your change. Just a moment, please. I'll wrap it for you.

47. Zhèlǐ yǒu gèzhǒng lǚyóu jìniànpǐn.
这里有 各种 旅游纪念品。
There are all kinds of souvenirs here.

48. Jīntiān wǒmen jiāng pǐncháng dào zhèlǐ de tèsè fēngwèi měishí.
今天我们 将 品尝 到 这里的 特色风味 美食。
Today we will taste local delicacies here.

49. Wǒmen shāngdiàn yǒu fēicháng duō de gōngyìpǐn, jǔ jǐ gè lìzi, lìrú mùdiāo、sīchóu、yínqì、pídiāo děng děng.
我们 商店 有 非常 多的工艺品，举几个例子，例如木雕、丝绸、银器、皮雕 等 等。
There are a lot of handicrafts in our shop, such as wood carving, silk, silverware, leather carving, to name just a few.

50. Nín kǎolǜ hǎo mǎi diǎnr shénme le ma?
您考虑好买点儿 什么了吗？
Have you decided what to buy?

Appendixes

51. 下面请大家品尝这一特色美食吧。
    Xiàmiàn qǐng dàjiā pǐncháng zhè yī tèsè měishí ba.
    Now please enjoy this hearty meal.

52. 境外旅行保险是针对国民境外旅游、探亲访友、公干面临的意外、医疗等风险联合推出的24小时全天候、综合性的紧急救援服务及意外、医疗、救援服务费用保险保障。
    Jìngwài lǚxíng bǎoxiǎn shì zhēnduì guómín jìngwài lǚyóu, tànqīn fǎngyǒu, gōnggàn miànlín de yìwài, yīliáo děng fēngxiǎn liánhé tuīchū de 24 xiǎoshí quántiānhòu, zōnghéxìng de jǐnjí jiùyuán fúwù jí yìwài, yīliáo, jiùyuán fúwù fèiyòng bǎoxiǎn bǎozhàng.
    The outbound travel insurance is a 24-hour, comprehensive emergency rescue service and insurance protection for accidents, medical and rescue service expenses jointly launched against accidents, medical and other risks for nationals traveling abroad, visiting relatives and friends, and on business trips.

53. 境外旅行保险基本可分为人身安全和财产安全两种。
    Jìngwài lǚxíng bǎoxiǎn jīběn kě fēn wéi rénshēn ānquán hé cáichǎn ānquán liǎng zhǒng.
    Outbound travel insurance can be basically divided into two types: personal safety and property safety.

54. 当游客在境外旅游期间出现行李丢失、被盗、游客意外伤病和死亡时，可向保险公司索赔。
    Dāng yóukè zài jìngwài lǚyóu qījiān chūxiàn xínglǐ diūshī, bèidào, yóukè yìwài shāng bìng hé sǐwáng shí, kě xiàng bǎoxiǎn gōngsī suǒpéi.
    When a tourist's luggage is lost or stolen, or a tourist is injured, sick or killed by accident during an outbound travel, he/she can claim for compensation from the insurance company.

55. 在境外购物消费可以用外汇、旅行支票或者国际信用卡。
    Zài jìngwài gòuwù xiāofèi kěyǐ yòng wàihuì, lǚxíng zhīpiào huòzhě guójì xìnyòngkǎ.
    You can use foreign exchange, traveler's check or international credit card when shopping abroad.

56. 外汇使用起来方便，手续简单。
    Wàihuì shǐyòng qǐlái fāngbiàn, shǒuxù jiǎndān.
    Foreign exchange is convenient to use, with simple procedures.

57. 但是，带外汇出境有一定的额度限制，携带现金，安全也是个问题。
    Dànshì, dài wàihuì chūjìng yǒu yídìng de édù xiànzhì, xiédài xiànjīn, ānquán yě shì gè wèntí.
    However, there are limits on the amount of foreign currency you can carry abroad and carrying cash with you is also risky.

58. 旅行支票币种多，金额较高，适合携带数量较大的金额，其使用也是没有期限的。
    Lǚxíng zhīpiào bìzhǒng duō, jīn'é jiào gāo, shìhé xiédài shùliàng jiào dà de jīn'é, qí shǐyòng yě shì méiyǒu qīxiàn de.
    Traveler's checks are available in a variety of currencies and in large denominations, and suitable for carrying larger amounts, and there is no expiration date for their use.

59. 信用卡提供的服务全面，携带安全，在境外消费可直接刷卡，还可以透支使用。
    Xìnyòngkǎ tígōng de fúwù quánmiàn, xiédài ānquán, zài jìngwài xiāofèi kě zhíjiē shuākǎ, hái kěyǐ tòuzhī shǐyòng.
    Credit cards offer comprehensive services, are safe to carry, and can be used directly for overseas purchases, with the option for overdraft.

60. 国际信用卡的申领需要的时间较长，手续较麻烦，对申领者的审查比较严格。
    Guójì xìnyòngkǎ de shēnlǐng xūyào de shíjiān jiào zhǎng, shǒuxù jiào máfan, duì shēnlǐngzhě de shěnchá bǐjiào yángé.
    Appling for an international credit card can be time-consuming and complicated, and the applicants will be examined strictly.

61. 下面我想提醒大家几点安全注意事项，希望我们拥有一个安全愉快的旅程。
    Xiàmiàn wǒ xiǎng tíxǐng dàjiā jǐ diǎn ānquán zhùyì shìxiàng, xīwàng wǒmen yōngyǒu yí gè ānquán yúkuài de lǚchéng.
    Now I would like to remind you of some safety precautions and hope that we can have a safe and pleasant journey.

62. 请大家严格按照旅行社的安排到指定餐厅用餐；不要暴饮暴食，以免水土不服引起腹泻。
    Qǐng dàjiā yángé ànzhào lǚxíngshè de ānpái dào zhǐdìng cāntīng yòngcān; búyào bàoyǐn-bàoshí, yǐmiǎn shuǐtǔ-bùfú yǐnqǐ fùxiè.
    Please dine at the designated restaurant by following the travel agency's arrangement strictly; do not overeat to avoid diarrhea caused by unacclimatization.

63. 请大家注意防护，避免蚊虫叮咬，以免感染登革热。
    Qǐng dàjiā zhùyì fánghù, bìmiǎn wénchóng dīngyǎo, yǐmiǎn gǎnrǎn dēnggérè.
    Please protect yourself from insect bites to prevent the risk of catching dengue fever.

64. 请大家自备防腹泻、过敏、感冒等常用药品，不要轻易将自己的药给其他游客服用。如确有需要，可拨打柬埔寨医疗急救电话119。
    Qǐng dàjiā zìbèi fáng fùxiè, guòmǐn, gǎnmào děng cháng yòng yàopǐn, búyào qīngyì jiāng zìjǐ de yào gěi qítā yóukè fúyòng. Rú què yǒu xūyào, kě bōdǎ Jiǎnpǔzhài yīliáo jíjiù diànhuà 119.
    Please bring some commonly used medicines to prevent diarrhea, allergies, colds, etc. for yourselves. Do not easily share your medicine with other tourists. If necessary, call the emergency medical service in Cambodia: 119.

65. 请确认自己的身体状态，身体不适或有心脏病、高血压、刚喝过酒、头晕目眩这些情况，禁止乘坐危险项目。
    Qǐng quèrèn zìjǐ de shēntǐ zhuàngtài, shēntǐ búshì huò yǒu xīnzàngbìng, gāoxuèyā, gāng hēguò jiǔ, tóuyūn-mùxuàn zhèxiē qíngkuàng, jìnzhǐ chéngzuò wēixiǎn xiàngmù.

Please confirm your physical status. You are prohibited from participating in dangerous activities if you feel uncomfortable, have heart disease or high blood pressure, have just drunk alcohol, or feel dizzy.

66. Zhèngquè zhuózhuāng, búyào chuān liányīqún, rénzìtuō, wúkòudài píxié.
    正确 着装，不要 穿 连衣裙、人字拖、无扣带皮鞋。
    Dress appropriately. Do not wear dresses, flip-flops, or leather shoes without buckles.

67. Zǐxì yuèdú yóukè xūzhī, liǎojiě guīzé, jìhǎo ānquán zhuāngzhì, bùdé zhōngtú jiěkāi shèbèi, bùdé xiédài yì rán yì bào wùpǐn rùchǎng.
    仔细阅读游客须知，了解规则，系好 安全 装置，不得 中途 解开 设备，不得 携带易燃易爆物品入场。
    Read the Notice to Visitors carefully to understand the rules, fasten the safety device, do not untie the device midway, and do not carry inflammables or explosives.

68. Yángé ànzhào zhǐshì jìnxíng cāozuò, fàngxia róngyì diàoluò de xiǎowùpǐn, rú yìngbì, yǎnjìng, shǒutíbāo, shǒujī.
    严格 按照 指示 进行 操作，放下 容易 掉落 的 小物品，如硬币、眼镜、手提包、手机。
    Follow the instructions strictly and remove small items that are apt to fall, such as coins, glasses, handbags and mobile phones.

69. Cānjiā shuǐshang xiàngmù shí, chuānhǎo jiùshēngyī; huáchuán, yóuyǒng, qiánshuǐ yídìng bù néng chāoyuè jǐngjièxiàn, búyào yuǎnlí rénqún, bìng tīngcóng jiùshēngyuán de zhǐhuī.
    参加 水上 项目 时，穿好 救生衣；划船、游泳、潜水一定不能 超越 警戒线，不要 远离 人群，并 听从 救生员 的指挥。
    Please wear life jackets for water entertainment activities, and do not go beyond the warning line when boating, swimming and diving. Do not stay away from other people, and follow the lifeguard's instructions.

70. Lǎorén hé xiǎoháir, yídìng yào liànglìérxíng, yǐmiǎn zàochéng yìwài.
    老人和小孩儿，一定 要 量力而行，以免 造成 意外。
    The elderly and children must act within their limits to avoid accidents.

71. Chéngzuò lǎnchē, mótiānlún shí, qǐng jiāzhǎng zhàogù hǎo zìjǐ de xiǎoháir, tóu, shǒu búyào shēnchū chuāng wài.
    乘坐 缆车、摩天轮时，请 家长 照顾 好自己的小孩儿，头、手不要 伸出 窗 外。
    When taking a cable car or sky wheel, parents should take good care of their children, and do not put your head and hands out of the window.

72. Xiàmiàn wǒ gěi dàjiā jiǎndān jièshào xiàr ××× xīyǐn yóukèmen de dìfang. ××× wénhuà jǐngguān shífēn fēngfù……
    下面 我给 大家 简单 介绍 下儿 ××× 吸引 游客们 的地方。××× 文化 景观 十分 丰富……
    Now I will give you a brief introduction to tourist attractions in ×××. ××× is abundant in cultural landscapes...

73. Chúle zhèxiē rénwén hé zìrán jǐngguān zhīwài, rúguǒ lái de zhèngshì shíhou, hái néng gǎnshòu xiàr ××× hěnduō jiérì huódòng, ××× děng.
    除了这些 人文和自然 景观 之外，如果来得 正 是 时候，还 能 感受 下儿 ××× 很多节日活动，××× 等。
    In addition to these cultural and natural landscapes, you can also experience many festival activities in ××× if you come here at the right time, such as ×××, etc.

74. ××× de chāoshì, cāntīng, jiǔdiàn děng dìfang dōu yòng měijīn jiào duō.
    ××× 的超 市、餐厅、酒店 等 地方 都 用 美金 较多。
    US dollars are used in most supermarkets, large restaurants and hotels, etc. in ×××.

75. ××× de shìchǎng děng dìfang dōu yòng dāngdìbì, jiànyì suíshēn dài shìliàng dāngdìbì.
    ××× 的 市场 等地方都 用 当地币，建议 随身 带适量 当地币。
    Local currency is used in markets and by vendors, etc. in ×××. You are advised to carry an appropriate amount of local currency with you.

76. Jìn fósì cānguān shí, yīzhuó détǐ zhěngjié, xū zhuó zhǎng yīkù, miǎnguān tuōxié.
    进佛寺参观 时，衣着得体整洁，需着 长 衣裤，免冠 脱鞋。
    When visiting a Buddhist temple, you should dress appropriately and neatly, wear long trousers, and take off your hat and shoes.

77. ××× shì yí ge xiǎofèi zhìdù guójiā, dāngdì jiǔdiàn hé sījī bāngzhù tí xíngli huò kèfáng sòngshuǐ, xiànhuā děng, ànzhào lǐmào shì yào gěi xiǎofèi de.
    ××× 是一个小费制度国家，当地 酒店和司机 帮助 提行李或 客房 送 水、献花 等，按照礼貌 是 要 给 小费的。
    ××× is a country adopting tipping system. The local driver and hotel staff who assist with luggage, deliver water to your room, or present flowers, etc., should be given a tip as a courtesy.

78. ××× duì zìrán de bǎohù hěn zhòngshì, gōnggòng chǎngsuǒ bù zhǔn xīyān, fǒuzé huì bèi fákuǎn.
    ××× 对自然 的保护 很 重视，公共 场所 不 准 吸烟，否则会被 罚款。
    The ××× attaches great importance to the conservation of nature. Smoking is not allowed in public places, otherwise you will be fined.

79. ××× guó jìn dǔ, jíshǐ zài jiǔdiàn fángjiān nèi yě qǐngwù jìnxíng dǔbólèi huódòng.
    ××× 国禁赌，即使在 酒店 房间 内也请勿进行赌博类活动。
    Gambling is prohibited in ×××. Do not engage in gambling activities, even in hotel rooms.

80. 夜间或自由活动时间若需自行外出，请告知领队，并应特别注意安全。
If you need to go out by yourself at night or during free time, please inform the team leader and pay special attention to safety.

81. 偷窃文物或破坏古迹，都是犯罪的行为，将受到法律制裁。
Stealing cultural relics or destroying historic sites is a crime and will be punished by law.

82. 有些国家当地人认为左手是不洁的象征，用左手拿东西或食物，都是不懂礼貌的表现。因此，请勿使用左手触摸或传递物品给当地人。
Locals in some countries believe that the left hand is a symbol of uncleanness, and it is impolite to use the left hand to hold things or food. Therefore, do not touch or pass things to locals with your left hand.

83. 您在旅途中碰到任何困难和问题请告诉我，我将尽力帮助您解决。
Please let me know if you encounter any difficulties or problems during your journey, and I will try my best to help you to solve them.

84. 现在大家可以自由参观，拍照留念，领略当地的风俗人情。
Now you can look around freely, take photos and have a taste of local customs.

85. 请大家在游玩时不要乱扔果皮和食品包装袋，不要到危险的地方去。
Please don't litter, and don't go to dangerous places.

86. 在这次×××之旅即将结束之际，我由衷地感谢大家对我工作的支持和帮助。
At the end of this ××× tour, I sincerely thank you all for your support and help.

87. 在这几天的旅程中，如果我们的安排和服务有不周到的地方，还请您多多包涵，同时也请您指出来，我们会努力完善。
Please excuse any shortcomings there may be during the journey, and we will try our best to make continuous improvement.

88. 像您这样有地位/成就的人……
A person in your position/high-achiever like you…

89. 如果您可以……我会很感激您。
If you could…I would appreciate it.

90. 也许您可以在……方面给我一些建议……
Maybe you can give me some advice on…

91. 您真的在……方面帮了我一个忙。
You really did me a favor…

92. 请您……因为您真的有这方面的专业知识。
Please… because you are a specialist in this field.

93. 您说得完全正确。
You are absolutely right.

94. 我为您所遇到的问题而感到非常抱歉。
I am very sorry for the problems you have encountered.

95. 请您不要着急，我非常理解您的心情，我们一定会竭尽全力为您解决的。
Please don't worry. I fully understand your feeling. We will try our best to solve the problem for you.

96. 我们会将您说的情况尽快反映给相关部门去做改进。
We will report what you've said to the relevant departments for improvement as soon as possible.

97. 谢谢您的理解和支持，我们将不断改进服务，让您满意。
Thank you for your understanding and support. We will continue to improve our service to your satisfaction.

98. 欢迎您和您的家人、朋友能再次到美丽的×××旅游！
I hope to serve you, your family and friends in the beautiful ××× again!

99. 最后，祝大家归途顺利，一路平安！
Finally, I wish you a smooth and safe journey home!

词语总表
Vocabulary

序号	生词	拼音	词性	词义	普通G/专业S	所属项目
1	安排	ānpái	n.	arrangement	G	5A
2	安全带	ānquándài	n.	seat belt	S	2A
3	保管	bǎoguǎn	v.	take care of	S	2B
4	保险	bǎoxiǎn	n.	insurance	S	4B
5	保证金	bǎozhèngjīn	n.	deposit	S	4A
6	报警	bào//jǐng	v.	call the police	G	4B
7	便携	biànxié	adj.	portable	S	3B
8	标志	biāozhì	n.	sign	S	2B
9	滨江公园	Bīnjiāng Gōngyuán	pn.	the Riverside Park	S	1B
10	不适	búshì	adj.	uncomfortable	G	5B
11	参观	cānguān	v.	visit	G	1B
12	餐厅	cāntīng	n.	restaurant	G	5A
13	车牌号	chēpáihào	n.	license plate number	S	2B
14	乘坐	chéngzuò	v.	take or ride	G	5B
15	充值	chōngzhí	v.	recharge	S	3A
16	出示	chūshì	v.	show	G	3A
17	出售	chūshòu	v.	sell	G	2B
18	搭乘	dāchéng	v.	travel by	S	2A
19	带领	dàilǐng	v.	take (sb.) to (a place)	G	1B
20	单价	dānjià	n.	unit price	S	3B
21	导游	dǎoyóu	n.	tour guide	S	1A
22	倒时差	dǎo shíchā	phr.	get over the jet lag	S	5B
23	抵达	dǐdá	v.	arrive	G	3A
24	地址	dìzhǐ	n.	address	G	1A
25	丢失	diūshī	v.	lose	G	4B
26	东七区	dōng qī qū	phr.	GMT+07:00	S	5A
27	独立纪念碑	Dúlì Jìniànbēi	pn.	the Independence Monument	S	1B
28	兑换	duìhuàn	v.	exchange	S	4A
29	反应	fǎnyìng	n./v.	reaction; react	G	5B

(续表)

序号	生词	拼音	词性	词义	普通 G/专业 S	所属项目
30	方式	fāngshì	n.	way	G	3B
31	付款	fù//kuǎn	v.	pay a sum of money	G	4A
32	赶紧	gǎnjǐn	adv.	quickly	G	4B
33	跟	gēn	v.	follow	G	1B
34	观察	guānchá	v.	observe	G	2A
35	贵重	guìzhòng	adj.	precious	G	2B
36	国籍	guójí	n.	nationality	S	1A
37	国际	guójì	adj.	international	G	5A
38	海关申报表	hǎiguān shēnbàobiǎo	phr.	Customs Declaration Form	S	1A
39	航班号	hángbānhào	n.	flight number	S	1A
40	护照号	hùzhàohào	n.	passport number	S	1A
41	集合	jíhé	v.	gather	G	2B
42	价格	jiàgé	n.	price	G	3B
43	监控	jiānkòng	v.	monitor	G	4B
44	柬埔寨	Jiǎnpǔzhài	pn.	Cambodia	S	5A
45	交通工具	jiāotōng gōngjù	phr.	means of transportation	S	2A
46	缴纳	jiǎonà	v.	pay	S	4A
47	解决	jiějué	v.	solve	G	5A
48	解释	jiěshì	n.	explanation	G	5B
49	金边	Jīnbiān	pn.	Phnom Penh	S	5A
50	金边王宫	Jīnbiān Wánggōng	pn.	the Royal Palace of Phnom Penh	S	1B
51	金额	jīn'é	n.	amount of money	G	3A
52	精彩	jīngcǎi	adj.	wonderful	G	5A
53	景区	jǐngqū	n.	scenic spot	G	2B
54	救生船	jiùshēngchuán	n.	lifeboat	S	2A
55	救生衣	jiùshēngyī	n.	life jacket	S	2A
56	剧场	jùchǎng	n.	theater	G	5A
57	扣除	kòuchú	v.	deduct	G	4A
58	牢记	láojì	v.	keep in mind	G	2A
59	理赔	lǐpéi	v.	settle a claim	S	4B
60	流量	liúliàng	n.	data	S	3A

（续表）

序号	生词	拼音	词性	词义	普通G/专业S	所属项目
61	旅程	lǚchéng	n.	journey	G	3A
62	旅行	lǚxíng	v.	travel	G	2A
63	旅行社	lǚxíngshè	n.	travel agency	S	4B
64	旅行支票	lǚxíng zhīpiào	phr.	traveler's check	S	4A
65	轮船	lúnchuán	n.	ship	G	2A
66	面额	miàn'é	n.	denomination	S	4A
67	灭火器	mièhuǒqì	n.	fire extinguisher	S	2A
68	明显	míngxiǎn	adj.	obvious	G	5B
69	目的	mùdì	n.	purpose	G	1A
70	期限	qīxiàn	n.	deadline	G	4A
71	其他	qítā	pron.	other	G	3B
72	签发	qiānfā	v.	issue	S	1A
73	签证	qiānzhèng	n.	visa	S	1A
74	全力	quánlì	adv.	try one's best	G	5A
75	荣幸	róngxìng	adj.	honored	G	1B
76	入住	rùzhù	v.	check in	G	5A
77	上网	shàng//wǎng	v.	surf the Internet	S	3B
78	设备	shèbèi	n.	equipment	S	3B
79	设施	shèshī	n.	facility	S	2B
80	申领	shēnlǐng	v.	apply	S	4A
81	审查	shěnchá	v.	examine	S	4A
82	生理	shēnglǐ	n.	physiology	G	5B
83	时差	shíchā	n.	time difference	G	5A
84	时区	shíqū	n.	time zone	G	5A
85	使用	shǐyòng	v.	use	G	3B
86	首都	shǒudū	n.	capital	G	5A
87	手续费	shǒuxùfèi	n.	service charge	S	4A
88	刷卡	shuākǎ	v.	pay by card	G	3A
89	索赔	suǒpéi	v.	claim for compensation	S	4B
90	套餐	tàocān	n.	package	S	3A
91	填写	tiánxiě	v.	fill in	G	1A

(续表)

序号	生词	拼音	词性	词义	普通 G/专业 S	所属项目
92	停留	tíngliú	v.	stay	G	1A
93	透支	tòuzhī	v.	overdraw	S	4A
94	外汇	wàihuì	n.	foreign currency	S	4A
95	外面	wàimiàn	n.	outside	G	4B
96	危险	wēixiǎn	adj.	dangerous	G	2A
97	卫生间	wèishēngjiān	n.	restroom	G	4B
98	吴哥窟	Wúgē Kū	pn.	Angkor Wat	S	1B
99	无证摊贩	wúzhèng tānfàn	phr.	unlicensed vendor	S	2B
100	现金	xiànjīn	n.	cash	G	3A
101	限制	xiànzhì	v.	limit	G	4A
102	相差	xiāng chà	phr.	differ	S	5A
103	消费	xiāofèi	v.	consume	G	4A
104	携带	xiédài	v.	carry	G	4A
105	信用额度	xìnyòng édù	phr.	credit limit	S	4A
106	信用卡	xìnyòngkǎ	n.	credit card	S	4A
107	行程	xíngchéng	n.	itinerary	G	1B
108	行程天数	xíngchéng tiān shù	phr.	days of (one's) travel	S	3B
109	休息	xiūxi	v.	rest	G	1B
110	押金	yājīn	n.	deposit	S	3B
111	严禁	yánjìn	v.	strictly prohibit	S	2B
112	演出	yǎnchū	n.	performance	G	5A
113	椅子	yǐzi	n.	chair	G	4B
114	易燃品	yìránpǐn	n.	inflammable material	S	2A
115	饮食安全	yǐnshí ānquán	phr.	food safety	S	2B
116	影响	yǐngxiǎng	n.	influence	G	5B
117	拥堵	yōngdǔ	v.	crowd	G	2B
118	用餐	yòng//cān	v.	have a dinner	G	5A
119	游览	yóulǎn	v.	go sightseeing	S	2B
120	游轮	yóulún	n.	cruise ship	S	2A
121	运营商	yùnyíngshāng	n.	operator	S	3A
122	正常	zhèngcháng	adj.	normal	G	3B

（续表）

序号	生词	拼音	词性	词义	普通 G/专业 S	所属项目
123	证明书	zhèngmíngshū	n.	certificate	S	4B
124	钟形塔	Zhōngxíng Tǎ	pn.	the Wat Phnom	S	1B
125	注意	zhùyì	v.	pay attention to	G	2A
126	租赁点	zūlìndiǎn	n.	rental point	S	3B
127	租用	zūyòng	v.	rent	S	3B

视频脚本
Video Scripts

项目一　出入境知识与手续

一、热身

　　红色通道也称"应税通道"。旅游团到达出境地点，首先办理海关手续，如有物品申报，要认真填写《海关进/出境旅客行李物品申报单》，走红色通道，办理海关手续，经海关查验后放行。

　　绿色通道亦称"免税通道"或"无申报通道"。携带无须向海关申报物品的游客和持有外交签证或礼遇签证的人员，可选择"绿色通道"通关。

三、视听说

　　安全检查是出入境人员必须履行的检查手续，是保障旅客人身安全的重要预防措施。安全检查的内容主要是检查旅客及其行李物品中是否携带枪支、弹药，易爆、腐蚀、有毒、放射性等危险物品，以确保航空器及乘客的安全。

四、学以致用

1.准备护照、签证和美元现金；2.填写两张柬埔寨提供的入境登记表，包括入境移民卡、海关申报表；3.如需办落地签，到达机场后，前往办理签证窗口办理，如已经办理签证，到入境处办理出关；4.提取航运行李。

项目二　旅游安全知识

一、热身

　　导游需要了解各种旅行时的安全知识，比如：提醒客人出入酒店房间请随手关门，勿将衣物披在灯上或在床上抽烟，这属于酒店住宿安全；外出时，不随意购买、食用街头小摊贩的劣质食品、饮料，这是购物饮食安全；在景区搭乘缆车时，请依序上下，听从工作人员指挥，这是景区游览安全；乘坐飞机时不能携带易燃、易爆、有毒物品，这是交通工具安全。

三、视听说

　　外出时尽量不要携带大量现金。参加水上活动，按规定穿着救生衣。旅行中带一些必备的药品。乘船时，不在船头、甲板等地打闹、追逐。酒店住宿时，听到火警铃响，请由紧急出口迅速离开，切勿搭乘电梯。搭乘缆车时，不能自行打开轿厢门或护栏，应听从工作人员指挥。

四、学以致用

带领游客游览景区：

1. 前往景区前，提醒游客贵重物品随身携带。提醒有门票优惠的游客，携带并出示学生证、老年证、离退休证、军官证、残疾证等有效证件。告知游客导游的联系方式及集合时间和地点，提醒游客记清所乘大巴的车牌号码、车辆名称和颜色特征。
2. 到达景区后，按照协议价购买门票，如遇儿童价不含景点门票、缆车需额外收费等问题，提前与游客沟通，协助游客办理票务等手续。
3. 游玩景区时，提醒游客注意安全。做好景点的讲解工作，合理安排游客拍照留念和休息的时间。提醒游客集合时间和地点。
4. 游玩结束后，查点和确认游客人数。发车前往用餐酒店前，提前联系和安排好游客的用餐。

项目三　出入境知识与手续

一、热身

　　Cellcard、Metfone 和 SMART 是柬埔寨主要的三大运营商。Cellcard 是柬埔寨品牌最大、用户最多的公司，在城市信号和通话质量较好，支持 4G。Metfone 是越南的品牌，信号覆盖面广，即使到偏远的乡村，信号也很好。Samrt 是一家年轻且发展迅速的马来西亚公司，备受年轻人喜欢，信号覆盖广，包括农村地区，支持 4G。

三、视听说

在柬埔寨使用网络可以购买当地电话卡或是租用便携式 WIFI。它们各自都有优缺点。当地电话卡有着信号稳定、价格便宜并且可以通话的优点，但需要游客用护照实名制购买。而便携式 WIFI 方便多人使用，节省成本，无限流量，但缺点是信号不稳定，需要定期充电，有押金，并且需要及时归还。

四、学以致用

尊敬的客人，您好！今晚我们将要入住的是位于金边的柬埔寨 XXX 酒店，酒店为您提供了全程免费 WIFI 服务，你可以时刻与好友保持联系。信号覆盖酒店餐厅、大堂、行政酒廊、游泳池等公共区域以及客房，您可以在酒店的任何位置畅快地使用 WIFI 网络。入住的客人使用手机打开 WIFI 上网功能，连接名为 "Cambodian XXX Hotel" 的 WIFI 信号，并在跳转页面中输入房号和办理入住的房客姓名，即可使用互联网了。

项目四　货币和保险知识

一、热身

境外旅行保险是针对国民境外旅游、探亲访友、公干面临的意外、医疗等风险联合推出的 24 小时全天候、综合性的紧急救援服务及意外、医疗、救援服务费用保险保障，基本可分为人身安全和财产安全两种。当游客在境外旅游期间出现行李丢失、被盗，旅游者意外伤病和死亡时，可向保险公司索赔。

三、视听说

不属于索赔范围的物品包括：
1. 首饰、现金、邮票、飞机票、护照等；
2. 假牙、假肢、隐形眼镜；
3. 金银、珠宝、古字画及古玩；
4. 行李物品的自然磨损、虫咬、变色、锈蚀或老化。

不属于赔偿范围的疾病包括：
慢性病、传染病、分娩、怀孕、流产及牙科疾病。

四、学以致用

游客张三即将前往柬埔寨旅行，出行前张三为自己买了一份出境旅游保险，该份保险涉及的保险责任包括意外伤害、突发急性病身故、住院医疗、门诊医疗、牙科门诊等内容，总保险费为 205 元人民币。

项目五　国际时差知识

一、热身

世界时区的划分以本初子午线为标准，从西经 7.5° 到东经 7.5°（经度间隔为 15°）为零地区。由零时区的两个边界分别向东和向西，每隔经度 15° 划一个时区，东、西各划出 12 个时区，全球共划分成 24 个时区，东十二时区与西十二时区相重合。相邻两个时区的标准时相差一小时。判断地区的时区是将该地区的经度除以 15，得到的商是几，就是第几时区，如果有余数，看余数是否是大于 7.5，如果大于 7.5，那就在商的基础上加 1。

三、视听说

以下方法可以减轻时差对人体造成的影响：
1. 旅行前调整好睡眠模式；2. 禁食；3. 服用碧萝芷；4. 调整光照时间；5. 保证第一晚的睡眠；6. 佩戴 RE-TIMER 眼镜；7. 选择合适的航班；8. 选择适合自己生物钟的目的地。

四、学以致用

在之前通过经度判断时区的基础上，遵循同减异加的原则，可以算出时差。"同"指同在东时区或同在西时区，则两时区相减；"异"则指一个在东区，一个在西区，则两时区相加。根据时差，可以遵循东加西减的原则，计算出所求时区的时间。即所求时区在已知时区东边，则在已知时区的时间上加上时差；若在西边，则减去时差。

参考答案
Reference Answers

模块二　导游专业知识

项目一　出入境知识与手续

一、热身

1. D　2. C　3. A　4. B
2. A：3 4
   B：1 2 5 6

三、视听说

1. ×　3. ×　4. ×　6. ×　7. ×

四、学以致用

1. D　2. A　3. C　4. B

项目二　旅游安全知识

一、热身

1. （1）B　（2）A　（3）D　（4）C
2. （1）D　（2）C　（3）B　（4）A

三、视听说

1. ×　5. ×　6. ×
正确方法：
1. 外出时尽量不要携带大量现金。
5. 酒店住宿时，听到火警铃响，请由紧急出口迅速离开，切勿搭乘电梯。
6. 搭乘缆车时，不能自行打开轿厢门或护栏，应听从工作人员指挥。

四、学以致用

1. B　2. A　3. D　4. C

项目三　通信知识

一、热身

1. （1）B　（2）D　（3）C　（4）A
2.

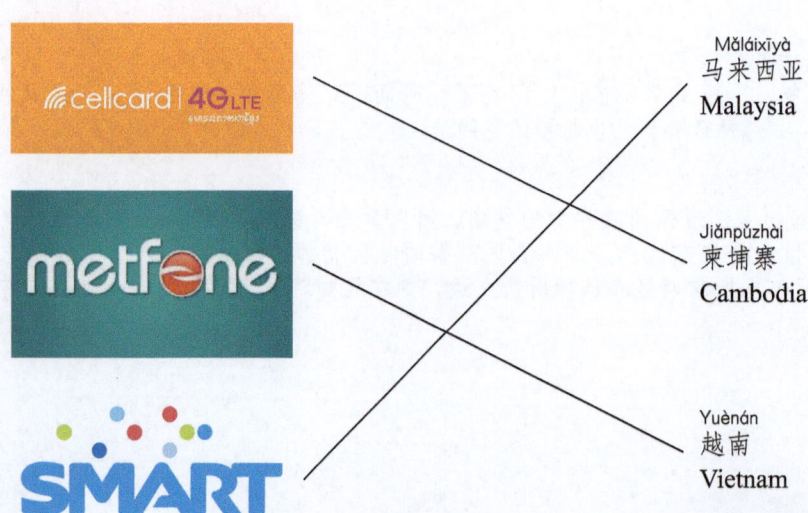

三、视听说

1. √   2. ×   3. ×   4. ×   5. √

四、学以致用

1. E   2. A   3. C   4. D   5. F   6. B

项目四 货币和保险知识

一、热身

1.（1）C （2）B （3）E （4）A （5）D （6）F

2. B   C   D

三、视听说

1. ×   2. ×   3. ×   4. ×   5. ×   8. ×

四、学以致用

1. C   2. A   3. D   4. B

项目五 国际时差知识

一、热身

1.（1）C （2）D （3）A （4）B

2.（1）东七 （2）东八 （3）东九 （4）零 （5）西五 （6）东二

三、视听说

tiáozhěng hǎo shuìmián móshì 1. 调整好睡眠模式 Adjusting sleeping mode	jìn shí 2. 禁食 Fasting	chíxù liáotiānr 3. 持续聊天儿 Keeping chatting	tiáozhěng guāngzhào shíjiān 4. 调整光照时间 Adjusting lighting time
√	√		√
tīng yáogǔn yīnyuè 5. 听摇滚音乐 Listening to rock and roll	chī xīnlà shíwù 6. 吃辛辣食物 Eating spicy food	pèidài re-timer yǎnjìng 7. 佩戴 re-timer 眼镜 Wearing re-timer glasses	xuǎnzé héshì de hángbān 8. 选择合适的航班 Choosing the right flight
	√		√

四、学以致用

1. 下午 7 点   2. 下午 8 点   3. 下午 8 点   4. 上午 6 点   5. 上午 11 点   6. 下午 9 点

模块四 导游专业实操

项目一 景区接待服务

流程与规范

A—3   B—4   C—1

工作模块一

quèrèndān
确认单
Confirmation Form

tuánhào 团号：20220212 Group No.	dìqū huò guójí Zhōngguó 地区或国籍：中国 Region or Nationality

中文 + 景点导游

cānguān rìqī 参观 日期 Visit date	jǐngdiǎn míngchēng 景点 名称 Name of scenic spot	rénshù chéngrén értóng 人数（成人/儿童） Number of people (adults/children)	yòngcān 用餐 Dining	bèizhù 备注 Notes
nián yuè rì 2022年2月12日 Feb.12, 2022	Wúgē kū 吴哥窟 Angkor Wat	rén chéngrén rén értóng rén 10人（成人6人，儿童4人） 10 people (6 adults, 4 children)	wǔcān, cānbiāo 12:00 午餐，餐标 rén $10/人 Lunch at 12:00, lunch standard: $10/person	rén bù chī là 4人不吃辣 Four people cannot eat spicy food
fèiyong héjì 费用 合计 Total Cost	$300			

工作模块二

1. __A__ 2. __D__ 3. __E__ 4. __B__ 5. __C__

6. __F__ 7. __H__ 8. __G__ 9. __J__ 10. __I__

11. __L__ 12. __K__ 13. __N__ 14. __O__ 15. __M__

工作模块三

diàochá xiàngmù 调查 项目 Survey item	hěn mǎnyì 很满意 Quite satisfied	mǎnyì 满意 Satisfied	yìbān 一般 So-so	bù mǎnyì 不满意 Not satisfied
wàibù jiāotōng zhǐyǐn 外部 交通 指引 External traffic guidance	√			
nèibù yóulǎn xiànlù 内部 游览 线路 Internal tour itinerary arrangement		√		
guānjǐng shèshī 观景 设施 Facilities for sightseeing		√		
lùbiāo zhǐshì 路标 指示 Signs for directions			√	
jǐngwù jièshàopái 景物 介绍牌 Introduction boards			√	
xuānchuán zīliào 宣传 资料 Publicity materials				√
dǎoyóu jiǎngjiě 导游 讲解 Tour guide service	√			
fúwù zhìliàng 服务 质量 Quality of service		√		

diàochá xiàngmù 调查 项目 Survey item	hěn mǎnyì 很满意 Quite satisfied	mǎnyì 满意 Satisfied	yìbān 一般 So-so	bù mǎnyì 不满意 Not satisfied
huánjìng wèishēng 环境 卫生 Environmental health			√	
yóukè fúwù zhōngxīn 游客 服务 中心 Tourist Service Center			√	
jǐngqū cèsuǒ 景区 厕所 Toilets			√	
shāngpǐn gòuwù 商品 购物 Shopping			√	
cānyǐn huò shípǐn 餐饮 或 食品 Food & beverage		√		
lǚyóu zhìxù 旅游 秩序 Public order				√
jǐngqū bǎohù 景区 保护 Scenic spot protection	√			
zǒngtǐ yìnxiàng 总体 印象 Overall impression		√		

qítā yìjiàn hé jiànyì：páiduì shíjiān tài cháng, méiyǒu dàigòu yǐnyòngshuǐ, xīwàng dǎoyóu nénggòu tíqián gàozhī zhùyì shìxiàng.
其他意见和建议：排队时间太长，没有带够饮用水，希望导游能够提前告知注意事项。
Other comments and suggestions: The queuing time was too long, and I didn't bring enough drinking water. I hope the tour guide can inform us of the precautions in advance.

项目二 景区解说服务

流程与规范
A—4　　B—3　　C—2

工作模块一

jǐngqū 景区	zìrán huánjìng 自然 环境 Natural environment	shèhuì huánjìng 社会 环境 Social environment	wénhuà huánjìng 文化 环境 Cultural environment	jīngjì huánjìng 经济 环境 Economic environment
Wúgē Kū 吴哥 窟 Angkor Wat			√	
Dònglǐsà Hú 洞里萨 湖 Tonle Sap	√			

（续表）

jǐngqū 景区	zìrán huánjìng 自然 环境 Natural environment	shèhuì huánjìng 社会 环境 Social environment	wénhuà huánjìng 文化 环境 Cultural environment	jīngjì huánjìng 经济 环境 Economic environment
Jiǎnpǔzhài 柬埔寨 Guójiā Bówùguǎn 国家 博物馆 National Museum of Cambodia			√	
Jújǐng 桔井 Kratie		√		√
Xīhānǔkè Hǎitān 西哈努克 海滩 Sihanoukville Beach	√			

工作模块二

1. B 2. E 3. H 4. A 5. J 6. G 7. C 8. I 9. D 10. F

工作模块三

2. √ 4. √ 5. √

项目三　景区商业服务

流程与规范

A—5　B—2　C—3　C—4

工作模块一

__C__ ⇒ __A__ ⇒ __E__ ⇒ __F__ ⇒ __G__ ⇒ __B__ ⇒
__I__ ⇒ __D__ ⇒ __H__

工作模块二

1. E 2. D 3. A 4. B 5. C

工作模块三

游客姓名 Tourist name	人数 Number of people	酒店地点 Hotel location	酒店房型 Hotel room type	特殊需求 Special needs
LI HUA	2	市区 In urban area	双人间 Double room	
WANG BIN	3	市区 In urban area	家庭房 Family room	
ZHANG QIANG	1	市区 In urban area	单人间 Single room	无烟 Non-smoking room
CHEN JING	2	郊区 In the suburb	双人间 Double room	安静 Quiet

项目四　其他辅助服务

流程与规范

A—3　　B—2　　C—4

工作模块一

cānguān lùxiàn 参观路线 Tour routes	cānguān shícháng 参观时长 Duration of visit	lùxiàn tèdiǎn 路线特点 Features of the route	shìhé rénqún 适合人群 Target tourists	jiāotōng qíngkuàng 交通情况 Transportation
线路一： 钟型塔＋滨江公园	2-3小时	全方位体验	中青年人	观览车＋步行
线路二： 钟形塔	1-1.5小时	山顶可参观塔山寺、俯瞰城区	中青年人	步行
线路三： 滨江公园	1小时	自然景观丰富、行程轻松	中老年人	观览车

工作模块二

1. B　2. D　3. E　4. A　5. J　6. G　7. C　8. I　9. H　10. F

工作模块三

yóukè 游客	cónglín fēiyuè 丛林飞跃 The jungle leap	jiǎnshì ànmó 柬式按摩 Cambodia massage	rèqìqiú 热气球 Hot air balloon	qiánshuǐ 潜水 Diving
yóukè 1～4 游客1～4				
yóukè 5～8 游客5～8	√			
yóukè 9～12 游客9～12		√		
yóukè 13～16 游客13～16				√
yóukè 17～20 游客17～20			√	

项目五　景点导游词学习

流程与规范

❶　C　　❷　D　　❸　B　　❹　A

工作模块一

1. 因为柬埔寨得艾滋病的人占百分之十五。
2. 因为别人认为灵魂在头上所以不要摸别人的头。
3. 因为当地有一种蚊子叫豹脚蚊，被咬之后会立刻死亡。
4. 因为当地的眼镜王蛇非常多所以要小心。

工作模块二
1. I 2. E 3. J 4. A 5. D 6. F 7. B 8. C 9. G 10. H 11. K

工作模块三
3. √   5. √

工作模块四
1. C 2. D 3. B 4. A 5. E